My name is Ralph Edwin Richey. Jonah in the Bible? If not, God in Nineveh. But Jonah ran from God he was sailing to Tarshish a great

the the men on the boat that it was because of his disobedience to the Lord that they were being swept up by the mighty storm, they tossed him overboard. Jonah was saved when a great fish swallowed him up. He remained safe in the belly of the fish for three days and three nights. After that, God commanded the fish to spit Jonah onto dry land. Jonah then went to Nineveh and preached the Lord's message to the Ninevites. Well, for the last two years the Lord has instructed me to go to Nineveh ( tell my story) but my foolish pride has prevented me from beginning this journey. I'm tired of running folks. My sons were taken from me almost 3 years ago and I haven't seen or talked to them since. I miss them like crazy and by the grace of God, I'm here to get them back. I'm sharing my story with the hope that someone, anyone, will read it and offer some advice on how to get my two sons, Mark and Robert back.

Like I said, my name is Ralph Edwin Richey but I go by Eddie Richey. I was born in Chattanooga, Tennessee, but was raised since age 2 in Spring Valley, California (a suburb of San Diego, California.) Being from the south, my Dad, Ralph Wilburn Richey gave me his first name as his first born son, but gave me a different middle name because he didn't want me to be known as Junior. He wanted me to have a real first name. So I was always known as Eddie. This caused me problems beginning at the time I entered kindergarten. I started school the first week and I was enjoying myself. On Thursday of the first week of school, my teacher phoned my Mom and said I had missed the entire week so far. My Mom came into my room frantic and said, "Eddie, where have you been going when I drop you off at school? I answered, "To class." She said, "When I take you to the class, where do you go?" I said, " To the circle." Because that's what we did. We would sit in a circle and play games. She was obviously getting frustrated. She yelled, "Where do you go?" I replied, "To take a nap." Here's what happened. When Mrs. Wright took roll, she would call out, "Ralph Richey." I would look around thinking my Dad was coming. I stayed quiet. I'm waiting for her to call Eddie Richey. To be honest, I thought my Dad was supposed to be there, but had to work. So I remained quiet. That's why she called that night. They finally got it all figured out and all the adults thought it was funny. I didn't! Up until that point in my life, when I made a mistake, I got my ass beat. I didn't understand it, but I sure wanted to know why I was going to catch this beat down. They explained it all to me and I was cool. But this was the first time I can remember getting in trouble for not doing shit wrong. But it wouldn't be the last! But no matter what...I would keep on smiling.

In 1980, my family and I moved about a mile away to Paradise Hills, California. It was a rougher neighborhood, with much more gang activity. I was playing baseball and basketball in high school. Since it was my junior year I was given the option to go to Morse High or remain at Mt. Miguel. Since I was already established at Mt. Miguel, I stayed there. I had gained a reputation as a pretty good athlete and known to have a good sense of humor. I did, and I still do. After graduation in 1981, I took a job at the local 7-11. About a month later, I was working overtime and it just happened to be the night that the San Diego Police Dept. went on strike. At 12:05 this big Warren Sapp lookin motherfucker walked in. He said, "You know the dogs are on strike right?" I said, "Yea, I heard that." Before I was even finished, he pulled out a .357 Magnum and put it in my face and said, "Gimme the money in that cash register motherfucker!" Shit, I couldn't get the money out fast enough, and I gave it to him. He grabbed it and hit the bricks. I stood there dumbfounded. I called my supervisor Rudy and he told me to call the police. I said, "I believe they are on strike." He said, "Fuck." Then he told me to wait for him, which I did. And customers kept coming in, so I just smiled.

Two weeks later, I was approached by Rudy at 7-11, he said he would give me a raise from $3.35 to $3.65 if I would work graveyard. I jumped at the chance. I began that night at 11:00 pm. Except for the fact that I couldn't sleep during the day, I had a blast working the night shift. My friends would come by and we would bullshit and basically have a party. About a week later, after my friends left, I was starting to clean up. At about 3:00 am, these two O.G.'s came in. One went to the cooler and the other went down one of the aisles. They both stepped up to the counter. The tall one placed a can of chili on the counter. I rang him up and he handed me a 10 dollar bill. I reached down to get a bag and this other motherfucker hit me in the back of the head with an unopened 7-Up bottle. I went down, but not out. The dude with the chili jumped on the counter and reached in to the register and just grabbed the whole til out. I regained my composer and busted his ass in the back of his head with a metal bar that we kept behind the counter. He grabbed his head but they both ran out. I stood there kind of dazed and then I phoned the police. I then called Rudy, and he said he was on his way. I sat there on the counter with 7-Up pouring off of my head. Right about then, this Barney Fife lookin Sheriff pops up in front of the store window with a sawed off shotgun. He was shaking like a son of a bitch and pointing the rifle at me. I don't know about you, but my instant reaction was to throw my hands up and yell, "I work here!" Not long after, Rudy showed up and he sent me home. When I got home, I woke my Dad and told him about it. He told me to take some Tylenol, get showered, and go to sleep. I showered and jumped in bed. I don't know if I was knocked out or sleeping, but about an hour later my Dad woke me up and said to get dressed. The cops had found the robbers. I got in a Sheriff's car and they drove me down the street. They had these two dudes under a street light. They shined a light on them and I told them that they were the guys. Just to be sure, I told the officer to check the tall dude's head because I know I cracked his ass good. They checked him and said he had a gash on the back of his head. Good! Sweet dreams motherfucker! And I kept on smiling.

Three weeks later I get a summons to appear in court to testify against the Chili Bandits. These were some ignorant fuckers. I had $19.00 in the register, but I still had the 10 dollar bill in my hand when they left. So they were facing armed-assault and armed-robbery for $9.00. And by the way, hell yea I kept the 10 dollars. Call it hazardous duty pay. I testified against them both and went home. I figured they would get some major time for this shit. Two weeks later I rode my bike to the store to pick up my check. When I reached the door, I hear someone say, "Hey Blood!" I turned around and it was Chili Dude getting out of a maroon Eldorado. I ran in the store, scared as hell, and grabbed the metal pipe. I went to the front door and opened it. He was standing in the parking lot. I said, "What Nigga?...this time I'm gonna ram this bitch through your heart." He just stood there, I figured if he was strapped I was going to die anyway so I might as well go out standing and not running around the parking lot, dodging bullets, like some Jackie Chan movie. He got back in the car and they left. That was my first experience with the inept California Justice system. But it wouldn't be my last. And they weren't going to take my smile.

I immediately went back to working the swing shift from 3 pm to 11 pm. One night I was working and my brother and another friend burst into the store and said they just saw on the news that the grunion were running that night down at South Mission Beach. They had already talked to this guy Henry that worked across the street at Mesa Liquor and he was down to go. I didn't know Henry well, but he was a nice guy and not only worked at the liquor store, but also at Von's Grocery store as a clerk. Henry and I both got off work at 11:00 pm. So I told my brother Charlie and Maurice to come back then. When they came back at 11 o'clock, I grabbed two tall cans of Budweiser and we all loaded into Henry's car. We drove to the beach with the windows rolled down and bumpin Teena Marie on the stereo. When we arrived at the beach we got out of the car and walked down to the beach. There was absolutely nothing happening down there. We kept walking and drinking our beers. Nothing! Me and Henry looked at Charlie and Maurice and said, "You're a couple of dumb motherfuckers." To this day I couldn't tell you what a fuckin grunion looks like. Dudes from the hood have no business at the beach at night. We walked back to the car, got in, and started back to Paradise Hills. We were hungry, so we stopped in Lemon Grove to get something to eat. We walked into Hogey's Corner, which was a little deli-style convenience store. We looked at the prices and then began pooling our money together. Between the four of us, we had 8 bucks. Obviously not enough for all of us to eat. Maurice said, "Let's go to Burger King." He insisted they were open 24 hours. So we got back into the car and rode down Broadway about a mile to the Burger King. Naturally, it was closed. Maurice was 0 for 2 and I told him to just, "Shut the fuck up!" Henry said, "Man, I'm going back to Hogey's and get some chips, then take you grunion huntin niggas home." We drove back down Broadway to Hogey's and pulled in the parking lot. When we came to a stop, 9 Sheriff's cars pinned us in and they all jumped out. What the fuck was this shit?! They were all screaming different things like, "Get your fuckin hands up, put your hands down, put your hands on the glass, don't fuckin move, move towards the door, open the damn door!" It was crazy. They opened the door and pulled us all out and slammed us on the hood of Henry's Dodge Charger. We're laying face down and I look over at Henry and say, "What the fuck is this?" He said, "Hell, I don't know!" This blond haired bitch cop put this little Dillinger-type pistol to the side of my head and said, "Shut up punk." I've always been deathly afraid of guns, so I promptly shut the fuck up. The reason I've always been afraid of guns is because when I was about 12, two of my cousins were hunting squirrels up on Dictionary Hill in Spring Valley. Somehow, my cousin Van dropped his pellet gun and it discharged. The pellet struck my other cousin, Aaron, in the corner of his eye. The paramedics rushed him to the hospital where they pronounced him dead. At Aaron's funeral I was shocked to see him in that casket with his orange hunting cap, vest, and his pellet gun draped across his chest. I touched him and he was cold. I vowed right then that I never wanted anything to do with guns. So anyway, a cop came over and took my wallet out of my pocket. I laid there for what seemed like forever. Then another cop grabbed me by my wrists behind my back, cuffed me, and threw me in the patrol vehicle. They eventually put Henry in the car with me and we drove to the Sheriff's station. When we got there they put Henry in one room, and me in another. My head was swimming, I couldn't figure out for the life of me what we could have done to earn this type of treatment. After about two hours this cop opened the door and led me into another room. He sat me down and said, "First of all, don't try to bullshit me. Henry already told us about the robberies." What?!! They had a report lately of, what they termed, a double-salt and pepper sticking up liquor stores. The report was of two black guys and two white guys doing the holdups. Now it was late, I was tired, and I wasn't all there but I'm also not a fool. They obviously had the wrong dudes and I was going to straighten this thing out as fast as I could. Hell, how could I rob someone when I was too busy getting robbed? I said, "Sir, I know that Henry didn't admit to any stick-ups, because we haven't done anything. Here's what I know, we stopped to get a snack on our way home from the beach. I work full-time at 7-11 and am enrolled at Grossmont College in the fall where I'm hoping to play baseball. Henry has two jobs and is known as a good guy in the neighborhood. That's it!" I felt I laid it out fairly well and this would all be over soon. The cop left the room. A few minutes later he came back in to retrieve his notebook and I said, "Can I leave now?" He looked over at me and quipped, "The only place you're going is downtown when we get a transport vehicle." Once again, What the fuck?!!! But that's exactly what they did. They took us to the downtown San Diego Jail on C St. At the jail, they told me that I was being charged with Possession & Manufacturing of Weapons. Huh? Say what? Oh hell no! When they put us in the bullpen I asked Henry, "What the hell are they talking about?" It seems that Henry had made a cast-iron, solid hand gun in metal shop at Morse High. He kept it under his car seat for protection. Protection? What are you going to do, throw the motherfucker at someone? They took me into a room and issued me my clothes and I got dressed. They took me up to the 3$^{rd}$ floor and stuck me in a cell with about 50 other dudes. I stayed there about 6 hours and saw one of the best fights I've ever seen. This little guy kicked the shit out of this huge dude. The big fool tried to punk the little dude and the little guy said, "Listen, you're big and you will fall hard." The big guy pushed the little dude and he got served up proper. That kid knew some tight-ass arts because when I left, Goliath still hadn't moved. I heard my name, and I went to the gate. An officer told me to roll up my mattress and stand by the gate. I came back with my shit and he led me into a room, I changed into my clothes, and they released me. I had been released on O.R. My Mom met me at the corner of C St. and we drove home. I learned that the only reason they took me and not Charlie and Maurice was because me and Henry were 18 years old. Ain't that a bitch?! My Mom said Charlie didn't really tell her anything. I couldn't believe that shit! He didn't explain that I really didn't do anything. That motherfucker just acted like, well Eddie was fucking around and got arrested. He thinks I forgot that shit, I haven't! He never offered to testify or even go to the attorney's office with me. My Dad woke me up the following morning and told me to get dressed. I asked, "For what?" He said we were going to see an attorney. I told him, "Dad, I didn't do anything." He said he knew that but we couldn't take any chances. We met with the attorney and I explained what went down. The attorney said he would take care of it. My Dad paid him $500 cash and we left. My Dad has never forgot that. Although my Dad always worked extremely hard as an Iron worker to take care of our family and is the most generous person I know, $500 bucks put a crunch on our family at that time. When we went to court on the matter, the fuckin Sheriff's Dept. didn't even show up. They fucked up and they knew it! The case was promptly dismissed. So my family is out $500 bucks and I have an arrest record for Manufacturing & Possessing Weapons, and those motherfuckers don't even have to issue me an apology? O.K., I see how this shit works. I smiled and looked forward.

I went off to college and played baseball for a year and a half. I completed 34 units towards my Associate's degree in Physical Education. I began fall practice in my second year but things were real tight at home so I dropped out and looked for a job. After some construction jobs came and went, I landed a job at Coca-Cola Bottling Co. in 1987. I was a merchandiser and ran a route in the North County which included Encinitas, Oceanside, Vista, Carlsbad, and San Marcos. I enjoyed the job and the pay but I hated that we started at 3:00 am. The route I ran was for the chain store accounts. At that time there was no such thing as a 24 hour grocery store. My job required me to build displays in the stores, so it only made sense to get in there during the time that they were closed to avoid being in customer's way while they shopped and it also helped me because I didn't have to worry about dropping six-packs or cases on the customers. I was working 12 to 15 hours a day there and really had no life. I met a girl named Julie in 1989. She had come from Nebraska to live with her father in our apartment complex. I had already made up my mind that I wasn't ever going to marry a girl from California because they all seemed to play too many games. We dated for about 2 months and she moved in with me. We lived together for about 3 months, when one night at a San Diego Padres baseball game I had the bright idea of getting married after a few too many beers. We went outside the stadium to a pay phone and looked up someone to marry us. We found a woman in Bonita, Ca. We phoned her and she said she could do it immediately. It was about 10:00 pm. We rolled up to the woman's house and got out of the car. We went to the front door and knocked. A woman answered and she introduced herself as Sherry Smith and she took us into her family room. She had everything ready and she married us. Just like that. We rode home to our apartment in El Cajon, Ca. I woke up the next morning and started trying to recall the previous night's events. I remembered the quickie wedding and felt that stomach pain you get when you realize you really fucked up. I looked over at Julie and thought how can we get this annulled and not create a scene? When she woke up I asked her if we really got married. I was hoping she would be equally as shocked, we would laugh, and we would make plans to get the farce annulled. I knew subconsciously that she drank too much (Bacardi and Coke-style drank) and had way too much mouth for us to ever stay together. She was overjoyed. Oh shit! This was the first time I ever put my wants and needs aside, even though it was the wrong thing to do, just to avoid hurting a woman's feelings. But it wouldn't be the last. We had a little reception at our apartment complex the following weekend. And that was that. Things went along for about 4 months and one Saturday afternoon while I was watching college football, we got into an argument and she stormed out of the apartment and went down to her Dad's apartment. She was gone about 2 hours, then returned to our place fired up. She had obviously went down to her alcoholic father's apartment and got good and oiled up on either Jack and Coke or Bacardi and Coke. I had locked the door when she left. She began banging on the door with her fists and kicking it. We had a sliding glass door next to the front door so I opened the blinds and saw the condition she was in. I told her to go away until she sobered up. She continued kicking the door so I opened the sliding glass door and told her to calm down. She said, in a slurring outrage, "Open the door you son of a bitch!" I said, "Not until you calm down." Right then she slammed her fist through the screen door and ripped the screen about three feet. I was holding her out as she tried to step through the screen. She was squirming and twisting, trying to force her way in, and she ripped the screen and it scratched her just below her left eye. She started jumping up and down and calling me every name in the book. I closed the sliding glass door and closed the blinds. I shouldn't of done that because now she was out of her fuckin mind. She went back downstairs to her Dad's house and I thought she would calm down, then we would talk. Wishful thinking! About 45 minutes later two El Cajon cops are knocking at my door. I let them in and they asked what was going on and I told them exactly what had gone down. They listened to me and then went back downstairs. I'm thinking, "Now you're in trouble you crazy bitch." They returned about 10 minutes later and told me to put my hands behind my back. What the fuck?! They handcuffed me and took me down the stairs. My twin nephews, who were coming to visit me were at the bottom of the stairs and they looked shocked. They said, "What happened Ed?" and I assured them I would be back soon. The cops took me down to the El Cajon station and placed me in a room. They left me there for about 2 hours and then came and got me. They said I was arrested for Domestic Violence but they weren't going to charge me because my wife was drunk. I was building an arrest record like some scumbag and I hadn't done shit! My Mom picked me up and took me home. I told Julie that either she was leaving or I would. She said she would leave and go back to Nebraska. And the next day, she did just that. I hate to admit it, but I smiled.

I continued working at Coke and was pretty pleased with my life at that point. One day I was moving some cases in the backroom of a Big Bear Market in Carlsbad and felt something pop in my lower back. My right leg went numb and I couldn't stand up. I called my supervisor and he told me to come back the plant. When I got back to the plant, they sent me to the hospital. The doctors took an x-ray and diagnosed me with a lower back strain. I was taken off work for a month and began seeing a chiropractor. Julie had been gone for about 2 ½ months. One day after I returned from the doctor, Julie called. This was the first time I had talked to her since she left. She said that she went to the doctor a few days earlier, they ran some tests, and that she was pregnant. Damn! My life had returned to normal and I was dating my chiropractor's assistant. I wish to this day that I would have stood my ground and told her that I would handle my responsibility, but in no way would I take her back. I knew that I would never forgive her for the domestic violence arrest. But no, my stupid ass told her to sell her call and make plane reservations. Man, for all I knew she could have went to Nebraska and got herself knocked up. But the idea of becoming a father really excited me. I picked her up, in the new car that I had purchased since she left, at the airport the following night. I took her home and tried to make the marriage work. My back was still sore and I had limited movement. This was before MRI's were common, so they kept giving me more medications. Finally, the doctors for Coke told me that they wanted to perform exploratory surgery and I said, "Hell No." Coke insisted that I have the surgery or I would be let go. I continued to balk and they fired me. I went to work for Budget Rental Car. On March 12, 1989 my son Eddie was born. I was still trying to make the marriage work (and so was she) but 6 months later it became apparent that a divorce was in order. I left our home, filed for divorce, and moved to Oceanside with my parents. It was the right thing to do, so I just smiled. Eddie went to live with her which killed me. I had really raised Eddie because Julie had no experience with infants. I had always helped out with my three nephews so I knew how to change diapers, feed him, bathe him, etc. She just let me do it and basically said fuck it. I surely didn't mind because I was so proud of this little guy and he was my pride and joy. We had a very strong father and son bond. But I accepted it and we set up a visitation schedule bi-weekly. I had started dating a woman from Oceanside named Martha. After dating 4 months, Martha and I planned a trip to Las Vegas. I know you're thinking, no way would this fool be stupid enough to jump back into a marriage. Yep, like an idiot, we got married at the Little White Chapel. She only had one requirement, that was that I had to move in with her immediately. Hmm, live with my Mom & Dad or move in with her? I think I can do that. So after a great weekend we drove home in wedded bliss. I moved in as promised and became step-dad to her 8 year old son Jarred. We were pretty happy, but there was one problem, my divorce from Julie wasn't final. We were certainly under the impression that it was. But this turned out to be a blessing. Since my ex-wife saw that we were stable throughout the past months, she offered to give me custody of Eddie before our final hearing. She was struggling, trying to party and date losers, so she didn't have time for Eddie. I was overjoyed! The divorce became final, we had custody of Eddie, and we went to a little place called I Do Weddings in Oceanside. We got legally married, and like I say, we were very happy. There were two problems though. She didn't want anymore children after she had Jarred. In fact she had her tubes tied after he was born to make sure of that. The other problem was that she never drank and she didn't want me to either. Now here she was with an infant son and Jarred, and I was occasionally drinking. I must say at this point that I can be very frustrating to anyone that has experienced problems in the past with someone that drank abusively, which she had in her first marriage. I can go months or years without touching a beer, so when I decide to have a beer, it's a major crisis for some people. Martha tried very hard to accept my occasional drinking and she was an excellent mother to Eddie, but she wasn't as happy as I was. We decided to divorce after 2 years and I was devastated. I was absolutely crushed! She moved back to her studio at her parent's home and I was left stranded with Eddie in our apartment. I had to call Julie and ask her to take Eddie while I got back on my feet. She was doing a little better at that time and she agreed to pick him up. I sat on the couch and looked into Eddie's eyes and said, "Honey, Mom is going to pick you up today and you're going to live with her until I can find us a place to live." He said, "Why can't we live here?" Holding back tears I said, "Because this place is too expensive." He got real quite, then said, "I'm worried Dad." I said, "About what?" He whispered, "About you." I started crying and told him, "It's just for a little while buddy, I'll be fine." Here I was thinking that I would have to console him and he was worried about me. I felt like a piece of shit! He looked up and said, "O.K., it will just be like a vacation, huh?" I said, "Yea." And we started packing up his belongings. I drove him to Poway and we met Julie. He looked over at me and said, "Just a little while, right?" and I said, "Yep, just a little while." He got into her car and off they went. As they passed me, I saw him waving at me, and it reminded me of the day I dropped him off at class on his first day of kindergarten. As I was walking by the class after getting him situated in the circle on the floor with the other children, I glanced into the window and he was waving at me. Just like that day, I broke down crying. I sat there and cried for what seemed like hours. I finally pulled myself together and drove home to pack. Half way there, I cracked a little smile. I gave away most of my things to my neighbors except my clothes, which I loaded in my car, and moved back in with my parents in Vista. It was then that I decided that I would quit drinking beer because it always seemed to be at the root of my relationship problems. I was tired of having these beautiful, laughter filled relationships that ended up being disasters over one argument. It always perplexed me that all the good times could be remembered as drunken horrors in the end. It wasn't fair, and certainly wasn't the truth.

One day, I went to the Vista Central Office of Alcoholics Anonymous and picked up a meeting schedule. I went home determined to attend that night. It was at 1450 E. Vista Way in Vista, Ca. The meeting was at 6:00 pm that night. My three nephews were out of school for the summer and were staying with us. I took them next door to the church to play stick ball. We were out there all day. I began to stress as the time got closer to 6:00 pm. I tried to enjoy my time with them, but the thought of the unknown occupied my thoughts. At 5:00 pm, we walked home and I got ready to leave to the meeting. I didn't want to go (kind of like the way I don't want to write this book) but I knew it was the right thing to do. I got into the car and drove out of the parking lot. I looked up, as I pulled out onto the street, and there it was! The address that I had going through my mind all day, 1450 E. Vista Way, was right there! I didn't even notice it all day. The church that we were playing ball at all day was where the meeting was. Wow! I pulled right in and went in to the meeting. The people there were so kind and made me feel so welcome. I heard men of every race, social background, etc. telling stories of their battles with alcohol and how they had overcome them. I listened intently and realized that I wanted what those guys had. My story was very light compared to most of them, but I knew that if it could work for them, it could work for me. I attended the meetings, got a sponsor, worked the 12-Steps of the program, and stayed sober for 3 years. After I was sober for about 4 months, my soon to be ex-wife, Martha, called me. She heard that I was going to A.A. and wanted to talk. I hadn't seen or talked to her since the day we split. The day that we did split, she got a restraining order against me. So I was kind of uncomfortable about going to see her. But if this was how we would reconcile, I figured I would give it a shot. I drove over to her house after church one Sunday and we sat down and talked. I spoke with her and her parents and it was very cordial. As I began to leave, I noticed a police car stopping in her driveway. Oh shit! She ran outside and went to talk to the officer. It seems that a guy she had been dating drove by her house and saw my car. He phoned the police and gave them the details of the restraining order. I went outside and spoke to the officer. She informed me that the restraining order was still in effect and to place my hands behind my back. As she was cuffing me, my soon to be ex-wife was yelling at the bastard that she had been dating, "Get the fuck out of here you piece of shit jarhead!" As we drove away, I could hear her screaming,

"Who the fuck do you think you are asshole?" When the officer and I got about a mile away, she pulled the car over and stopped. Since I was dressed in my church clothes, I guess she figured I just didn't look the part of a dangerous individual. I told her the story and she said, "What a bitch." As we rode to the Vista Jail, she told me that this wasn't very serious and I should be out in a couple of hours. I was booked into the jail for Violating a Restraining Order. The officer, Candy, gave me a hug, wished me luck and left the jail. I called my friend and he bailed me out within a couple of hours. The charges were dropped later on, and that was that. A few months later I read in the paper that Officer Candice Brown was shot and killed by an ex-lover in an apparent lover's triangle dispute that went terribly wrong. Yep, that was Candy, and I felt so bad because she was so kind to me the day she arrested me. Needless to say, I divorced Martha and I never saw or heard from her again. Yet another set back, and yet another smile. Nothing or no one will take my joy, period.

I continued working the 12-Steps of Alcohol Anonymous, attending meetings, and staying sober. One day I was looking through the newspaper and saw an add in the help wanted section for a baseball coach at Oceanside High School. I talked to the Athletic Director, Pat, and he said to come in for an interview with the Head Varsity Baseball Coach, Dave Barrett. I knew when I met Dave, we would be good friends. He was an ex-catcher that graduated from Oceanside High and Cal-Lutheran University. He had graduated from high school, went off to college, graduated, and came back to teach and coach at his Alma Mater. Man, this guy was actually living the vision that I always had for myself. Not to mention, he was an excellent role model for the kids. He is a devote Christian and a man of unshakable integrity. O.K., let me get off his jock and continue with the story. Dave hired me on the spot to coach the freshman team at Oceanside High. I worked with the youngsters and we began play in the Avocado League. Three games into the season, we traveled to Ramona High to play the Bulldogs. In the sixth inning, my player Chris Stewart was on third base in a tie ballgame. The pitcher for Ramona skipped one past the catcher to the backstop. I sent Chris home and he slid headfirst. The pitcher, covering home, caught the relay from the catcher and tagged him on the helmet. The umpire called him out. What?! I ran down the line to home plate and confronted this blind bastard. I got in his face and said, "You have to be kidding me. You know you missed this one, huh?" He said, "It is what it is Coach." I was furious, but I kept my composer and asked, "Where did he tag him?" The ump said, "On the helmet." I replied, "He slid headfirst, right?" Mr. Blue answered, "Yep." Now I had him, I said, "Are you telling me that he slid headfirst, was tagged on the head, and his hands hadn't reached the plate first?" He looked me straight in the eye and had the nerve to say, "You got it." I whispered, "You're out of your fuckin mind Skippy. Think about what you just said and tell me you're right." At that, he turned around and walked back to the edge of the backstop, picked up his water cooler, and started walking out towards the parking lot. I couldn't believe what I was seeing. This asshole was just going home. I walked next to this idiot all the way to the parking lot. I was pleading with him to stop. I said, "Don't do this to my kids, hey I'm an asshole, but don't make them suffer." He got in his car and drove away. I had never seen anything like this in my life. I went back to the field and the Ramona coach, who was a friend of mine, was laughing his ass off. I smirked and gave him a wave. I told my players to go up to the varsity game and come back to the bus when the game was over. I sat in the bus feeling like a total piece of shit. How do I explain this to my players? I couldn't very well tell them what I really thought. Which was, that fuckin umpire was a fuckin weak worm and should never work another game because he was a pussy! This game takes intestinal fortitude and if you don't have the guts to cope with the ups and downs of it, stay the fuck away. No, I had to find a way to explain this with tact. My mind was swimming. I'm very rarely at a loss for words, but I was. I came to the conclusion that the only way to handle this was to accept all the blame and move on. I saw the kids walking towards the bus, so I braced myself. When they all got on the bus, I stood up and addressed them, "Listen guys, you battled hard today and I had no right to take away from your effort. The fact of the matter is, I misread that umpire. I can usually tell who to speak to harshly and who to go easy on. I was wrong, and I apologize. I would only hope you treat me like I treat you when you boot a ground ball, drop a fly ball, or swing at ball four. I cost us a ballgame and that's on me. I can promise you that it will never happen again. Thank you for busting your tails today." And I sat down. We rode back to Oceanside in silence. I was still kind of beating myself up when I got off the bus. I was unloading the gear when my catcher Bobby Cruz walked up and said, "Coach, you didn't cost us that game. That pitcher was a scrub and we should have lit him up all day. It shouldn't have been close. We appreciate that you stand up for us." I said, "Thank you Bob, see you Monday." I got the gear put away, walked to my car, and drove home with tears in my eyes and a smile on my face.

On Monday, Dave called me into his office to chat. We talked about the game on Friday at Ramona and he had an idea. First, I needed to write a letter to the commissioner of C.I.F and apologize. Then he wanted me to be his assistant on the varsity team. Dave and I have that competitive gene that makes us appreciate passion for the game. I agreed, wrote the letter, and became his assistant. Things were going great, I had a great relationship with the players and we always had fun. I could still play the game at that time and I joined an adult league. I played for the Indians on Sundays. One of my teammates on the Indians named Elliot was working as the National Sales Manager for a printed tape company located in San Jose, CA. He gave me a ride home from our game one Sunday and asked me if I wanted to be his assistant at work. Besides coaching at the high school, I wasn't doing anything. I inquired as to what I would be doing and he said to meet him at his office in San Clemente, CA the following day. I showed up the next day at his office and quickly realized he really didn't do anything but run his damn mouth all day. He wasn't prospecting customers, building business relationships, or doing anything but acting like a big shot. By the third day I knew he was totally full of shit. I went in to his office on Thursday prepared to tell him that I wasn't interested in working for him and to pick up the money he owed me for the past three days. When I got there, all hell had broke loose. Elliott was yelling at the top of his lungs while on the phone with the President of the company, Robert. Elliott threw the phone down and stormed out of the office. I picked up the phone and said, "Hello." Robert was still on the line. He said, "Who is this?" I said, "It's Eddie." He asked me if I had any sales experience and I told him yes. He said, "Eddie, do me a favor. Take the computer, the phones, any company documents that you think might be useful, and all the company binders and put them in your car. If you're interested , you are now the National Sales Manager for my company." I was shocked! I went outside and tried to talk to Elliott, but he was storming around like a caged tiger and kicking everything he could find. I told him that Robert just offered me his job. He said, "You're not going to do it are you?" I stumbled around for an answer and finally said, "Well I do need a job." He said, "You motherfucker, you're a traitor." I said, "But this motherfucker has a job bitch, what do you have?" He walked towards his car, turned around and shouted, "I'm going to lunch, I'll be back and you better have changed your mind." Elliott peeled out of the parking lot like a NASCAR pro. I chuckled like a school girl, and immediately began loading up all of the office equipment that Robert instructed me to. When I got home, I called Robert and he told me that he and his wife, Kim, would be down to my house on Saturday to make me an official job offer. On Saturday, Robert and Kim came to my house and I officially became the National Sales Manager for Custom Printed Tape or better known as CPT. I agreed to a fair starting salary and was promised a generous commission package if I signed any new clients. We drove to Office Depot and purchased everything I needed to set up an office at home. I must mention that in 6 months, Elliott only booked 2 new customers. That's it. I was sure that I could top that pitiful effort. On Monday I hit the ground running. I thought, where can I go to find companies that use printed tape? It's the tape that company's use to seal their cardboard boxes. We printed on beige kraft tape or clear tape. I figured that the best place to find card board boxes was at the recycling plant. I went there and talked to the manager. I promised to bring him a 12 pack of beer every Friday if he would let me troll around his card board refuge pile. He said that would be fine. So I went to my car, got a razor knife, and started rummaging around the card board stack. It was great! When I found a piece of card board with printed tape on it I would cut the tape off and stick it in my pocket. Before I knew it, my pockets were stuffed with leads. I went home and emptied my pockets. The great thing about it was most of the tape samples had the companies name, address, and phone number on them. I picked up the phone and started dialing the numbers. When I reached them I would ask for the purchasing department or the purchasing agent. It took some getting used to, but I became pretty good at reaching the individual that was in charge of purchasing. I explained what we did and that I would like to give them a quote on their printed tape. If they agreed, I would get their particular usage amount for a month or year and I would forward the information to Robert. Now you must understand, Robert is not a real intelligent dude. He's an ego-driven manipulator that really doesn't know his head from his ass. The packaging company that he presided over was his wife's family's company. He had bullshitted them into believing he could manage the entire operation. But what he really cared about was the printed tape division so he could look like a big shot at their local tennis club. But anyway, when I would forward the information to Robert he would low-ball the competition. He didn't give a shit about profit margins or anything else. He just wanted to say that he held contracts with major corporations. I would then turn around and deliver the quotes to these companies and we would secure purchase orders for yearly amounts. That worked great and I was putting together quite an impressive portfolio. As time went along, I developed a good reputation, by word of mouth, and we no longer had to low-ball the competition. I built up a client base of such companies as Levi's, Van's Shoes, Subaru of California, Warehouse Records & Tapes, etc. In a couple of years I had built up 1.4 million worth of residual business for CPT. At the end of the year, all I would have to do was fax my clients a new contract and they would fax me back a purchase order for the following year. That was it! I would constantly talk to Robert about the supposed commission package that he promised me, but he would blow me off or just say later. The guy was a clown and I knew it. But I had to admit that I made pretty good money with my salary, and the job also provided me an opportunity to continue coaching at Oceanside High. At the time, my best friend Robert Hock, would constantly tell me that I needed to get a contract from CPT and establish an exact commission schedule. Hock is an excellent businessman in New York, and I knew he was right, but I didn't want to jump the gun because I had it pretty good. I had moved into my own condo which my neighbors called the "Stabbin Cabin" because I was seeing a lot of different women at the time. I drove a new car, had great furnishings in my home, and was living a great bachelor's life. I also had bi-weekly visitations with Eddie and we did everything like go to Disneyland, Sea World, minor league baseball games, etc. So it was all good. We had just the completed the baseball season at Oceanside High so I had my afternoons free. One day a friend of mine, Diane, called and said she wanted to introduce me to a friend of hers at work named Maritza. We decided to meet for dinner at Dalton's Roadhouse. When I arrived and met her friend, I knew right away that she wasn't my type. I prefer an L.A. face and an Oakland booty. She was thin as a rail and had a pitted face from severe acne. We finished dinner and went to a movie. I hugged them both goodbye after the show and drove home. Not happenin! For the next few weeks I worked diligently to prospect new clients at work. Since baseball was over I decided to work late most days. I was going out at 7:00 in the morning and often times not returning home until 10:00 in the evening after attending A.A meetings. One Friday night, Diane called. We chatted for a while and she mentioned that Maritza had drove up to Vista to spend the night with her. Somehow, Maritza ended up on the phone and she was talking like a straight ho. I don't know if she had been drinking, but I said fuck it and started spittin mack lines at her. Hook, line, and sinker...she was on her way over to "watch a movie." Shit, we got to the part in "My Cousin Vinny" where they are shopping in the grocery store for snacks, and we were knockin boots! When we were done, I said to her, "I'm going out." She answered, "O.K. Just give me a minute to get dressed." I said, "You don't have to leave." She replied, "You want me to stay here alone?" I realized what was going on and I told her that I meant I was going to sleep. We laughed and went to sleep. In the morning she left and I didn't expect to ever see her again. I wouldn't be so lucky.

It was Monday morning and I woke up early. I took a shower and got dressed. I picked up my phone to call a client and the phone was dead. What the fuck? I looked at my cell phone and it was dead too. I knew what was going on but I didn't want to accept it. I drove to the local 7-11 store and went to the pay phone. I called Robert in San Jose and it was just as I expected. That son of a bitch had fired me. I kind of knew something had to give because I had contracted too much business for this small time chump. He only had 2 printing machines and they were running day and night. He couldn't handle anymore business and he had figured out that he could call my clients just as easily as I could to get them to re-sign for another year. I had become expendable. Damn, I was livid! Why didn't I listen to Hock? I called the CPT office again hoping to speak to Robert's wife Kim and was told she was out of town. Shit, that's right, she had just told me a couple of days prior that she was going to Hawaii to get away from the childish punk she was married to. Kim and I always had a great relationship. She was a kind woman who came from a decent family and was starting to realize she married a piece of shit. Her words. Robert had the secretary tell me that I needed to return all CPT belongings before he would send my final check. He didn't have the balls to speak to me personally. I spent the rest of the day boxing up all of the company's materials. I absolutely seethed the entire time I did it. That night I went over to my parents house and told them the story. I used their phone and called Robert at home. This wasn't unusual since I spoke to him at home on a daily basis. I called and got the answering machine. After the beep I said, "Robert, you're a weak motherfucker and a piece of shit. That's why you're wife is in Hawaii without your miserable ass. Even she doesn't want to be around your slimy ass. I've packed up all company material and as soon as I receive my check, I will return it to you. Have a nice life you fat bastard!"

I went home and contemplated what I was going to do now. As I laid in my recliner, there was a knock at the door. I opened the door and there was Maritza. I told her that I was having a bad day and wouldn't be very good company. I had never called her since we were together and didn't intend to. That happens sometimes. She said she had a bad feeling all day that I was in trouble. I let her in and explained my frustrating day. She was very understanding and listened real intently. Hell, after the day I had, I needed some company. She made me dinner and I relaxed for the first time all day. We talked late into the night. She ended up spending the night and left for work early the next morning. At this time, I was in constant pain daily. See, about 4 months earlier, I was hit from behind by an elderly woman while on the way to the recycling plant. I told Robert immediately, but he said to please do him a favor and go through the woman's insurance. I agreed like a dumb shit! The woman hit me while I was stopped to make a left turn. She was traveling about 50 mph and hit me square. I had a fitted hat on and it was resting in my back window after the crash. My neck ached but I refused any medical attention because the woman was so upset because her airbags had deployed and she was real shaken up. I was worried about her. So I had been going to the doctor for the past 4 months and the pain was getting worse and worse. My insurance finally approved an MRI and it revealed two herniated disks at C-3 and C-4 in my neck. The woman's insurance paid to replace my car which was totally wrecked, but not my medical bills. As with most HMO insurance plans, they took the absolute conservative approach and did as little as possible. I couldn't stomach the pain pills so I was just left to suffer until the next authorization could be approved. After the MRI, I was approved for facet block injections. They would work for about a week, but then the pain would return. Eventually I had nerve denervation in the two areas which required surgery to laser the nerves leading to the painful areas. Luckily it worked, but it was a bitch. It was onwards and upwards and my smile remained in tact.

I decided to file a Workman's Compensation case against CPT. I went and got all the information and contacted an attorney. I spent most of my time documenting the events that took place while I was employed by CPT. One day I was writing and I looked out my window and saw Maritza carrying a box down the walk way. I went outside and followed her to the unit across from mine. I met her underneath the stairs and said, "What's up?" She said proudly, "I just rented this place and I'm moving in. Isn't that great?" Whoa! This was going to shake up my mack game. The "Stabbin Cabin" wasn't open 24/7 anymore, but it was still open! I said, "Why would you want to live up here when you work down in San Diego?" She said, "I want to be close to you." I thought "Fuck Me" but I smiled and offered to help her move.

She declined and told me her family was there to help her. I looked out in the parking lot and it looked like it does at Home Depot early in the morning. Her whole family was moving boxes like a trail of ants. Her mother walked by me and said, "Hola." I said, "What up?" Damn, this shit wasn't happening! But sure enough, she moved in within 4 hours. I went home, turned on the stereo and started bumpin some jams. If I would have had any balls, I would have called one of my A-frame tricks and let it be known that you can't stop a player, you can only hope to contain him. But no, my punk ass invited her and her 2 year old son, Michael, over for dinner. I sure wasn't going over to her house for dinner. From what I saw she had a television, a couch, and a bed. No thanks! So that was game, set, and match. I had a girlfriend. Hey, it's my fault. I made the decision to give up my freedom and settle in to this relationship. One morning she and I got into an argument and I told her it was over and left her place. I was home for a couple of hours and a police officer knocked on my door. When I answered the door he said, "Do you have a girlfriend that lives next door? I said, "Not anymore." And I meant that shit! He replied, "Well, do you know Maritza?" I said, "Yes." He said, "She has tried to commit suicide and has been rushed to Palomar Hospital." My heart about stopped. I said, "Is she alright? He said, "She looked pretty bad when they loaded her." I thanked him and ran to my car. What have I done? I was shaking as I drove to the hospital. I got there and ran in. I asked if she was there and they directed me to a room down the hall. I burst into the room. Damn...there she was laying on a table, looking half dead. There was black ash running down the side of her mouth. Again, what have I done? I went up to her and shook her and said, "Mitz, honey what did you do?" She was out of it big time. She didn't respond. I just crumbled. I just sat down and cried. A nurse came in after a few minutes and told me that the black ash was from the charcoal where they pumped her stomach. She had taken a whole bottle of Xanax. She went on to explain that she would be alright, and that it would just take a few hours for her to shake it off. Thank God! As I walked out, a mental health worker stopped me, and told me to make sure that I make Mitz an appointment as soon as possible for counseling. She looked me in the eyes and said, "No matter what she says, she's not well, OK?" I nodded and thanked her. I drove home feeling guilty as hell and promised myself that I would take care of her. My player days were over and this shit wasn't a game. Where I'm from we are tough, but we aren't cruel. Straight up! I went home and took a nap. Mitz called that night and asked if I would come get her. I told her I would be right there. I went to the hospital and picked her up. We drove home in silence. I put her to bed and sat up all night. Yep, this too shall pass, and I smiled.

Mitz seemed to get better. I broached the topic once about her getting help with some form of counseling. She got real upset and told me to mind my business. I left it alone. She never shared with me the fact that these types of episodes were common in her life. She had been hospitalized throughout her life for various mental health issues. That wasn't the first time she had weakly attempted suicide. The fact was, she took the pills then immediately called 911. That is not a person that truly wants to end their life. So I let it go for the time being. We continued to live together and things calmed down as long as I didn't challenge her on any major issues. I learned that one night about 5 months later. We got into an argument and she stormed out of the house. I had to stay home with her son Michael, so I couldn't very well chase after her. Her anger was so intense and it wasn't difficult at all to set her off. I stayed with Michael while she was out doing who knew what. About 2 hours later there was a knock on the door. I thought, Fuck not again, as I looked through the peep hole and saw a uniformed officer. When I opened the door the cop said, "Here's your girlfriend, she's having a rough night." Right then, Mitz stepped from behind him, eyes bloodshot, and stumbling. She walked into the house and went straight to our room. I stepped outside to talk to the officer. He said he found her sitting in her car down the hill, she was drinking wine, and crying uncontrollably. I told him that we had an argument and she left the house and left her son with me. That's why I didn't come looking for her. He wished me luck and left. I went in the house to tuck Michael in and then I laid on the couch in the living room. I was out of answers. How do I handle this insanity? I hadn't drank in over 4 years and here I was caring for someone who obviously needed professional care. Damn, I had been on anti-depressant medication for over 2 years. Why can't this bitch at least look into some form of treatment? I decided that I was done. In the morning I was going to confront her and tell her that if she didn't seek treatment I was gone. Period! And that's exactly what I did. When she came into the living room the following morning I told her we needed to talk. I just laid it out point blank. She agreed to make an appointment with her therapist that she had seen, off and on, for the past 8 years. What the fuck?! You have a therapist and have been putting me through this bullshit all this time? I held my tongue, but I wanted to tell her to get the hell out of my life. I was so stupid. She began seeing her therapist, got on medication, and things began getting better. That shit wouldn't last. We decided to move to an apartment in Escondido, Ca. It was in a rough part of town, but it was cheaper and we needed cheaper at that time. I was still waiting for my Worker's Compensation hearing against CPT and my disability payments were running out. Shortly after we moved, I received the letter that I had been waiting on for months. I had my hearing date. I spent most of my time documenting the final details of my time at CPT, and going to consult with my attorney. My attorney was confident that we would prevail so I was feeling very upbeat. The day came for my hearing and I put on my best suit and shined my shoes. Besides Mitz, my Mom and my Dad went with me to the courthouse. As I walked upstairs I saw Robert's fat ass. What a fuckin worm! He got up and ran towards the back of the building, as if I was going to jeopardize my case by kicking his ass. The guy is a clown I tell you. My attorney and I went into the hearing which lasted about 45 minutes. We described my employment with CPT, the sales that I secured for the company, the accident that I was involved in, and the way I was terminated by them. Robert really had no defense. It was obvious that I was treated wrong and eventually was screwed by him and his company. As well as it was going for me, I couldn't understand why Robert seemed so relaxed and confident. I mean, it had to be a hassle to drive the 8 hours down here to San Diego from San Jose, the facts that we were describing were making him look like a pure slime ball, and he really never denied anything that my attorney accused him of. What the hell was this bastard up to? During the final 10 minutes of the hearing, I kept noticing a California Highway Patrol officer walking past the door. He would look into the room and then keep walking. I looked around the room, who was he looking for? Was someone double parked? Did he have a Worker's Comp case too? I was trying to put this together. When the hearing ended, my attorney and I walked out the door into the hall and he said, "Well, you did it kid. Congratulations. He had no legal leg to stand on. We should have a decision in your favor shortly." We shook hands and started for the elevator. Out of the blue, I felt a hand on my shoulder and I turned around. It was the CHP officer and he said, "Are you Ralph Richey?" I said, "Yes I am." He replied, "Mr. Richey, I have an arrest warrant for you out of Santa Clara County, please place your hands behind your back." I put my hands behind my back and thought No fuckin way! The officer led me towards the elevator where my parents and Mitz were standing. They were all saying, "What's going on?" I said, "I don't know!" The officer said, "He's being arrested."

My Dad said, "Well no shit buddy, but why?" The officer didn't respond. We went down the elevator and to his car. What did I NOT do this time?! When we got to the jail, which was just around the corner, I saw a friend of mine that I had grown up with and played recreation league basketball with. His name is Scott and he works for the Sheriff's department at the jail. I said, "What's up Scotty?" He said, "Nice suit Ed, what's going on?" I answered, "I have no fucking idea." He said if he found out anything he would come tell me in the bullpen. I was only there for about an hour and was bailed out by my family. Scott never did come tell me anything, so I left the jail knowing nothing at all. When I met my family on the street my Dad told me, as we walked to the car, that Robert had pressed charges against me in San Jose for my message that I left on his answering machine the day he fired me. I told my Dad that I didn't threaten the guy or anything, but only called him a fat bastard and a piece of shit. Which the motherfucker is! Freedom of speech, right? Wrong! It seems that it is a misdemeanor to leave a message on someone's answering machine that includes foul or vulgar language. Hell, who knew? I have 2 ex-wives that did it on a regular basis. You really have to keep up with Civil Law in the State of California. The place is financially supported by the jails, the prisons, and the joke of a justice system. So here I was, doing my part to contribute to the bullshit. You're welcome motherfuckers!

Around a week later I received the decision of my Worker's Comp case. I lost. Seems when you get arrested after your hearing it sways the judge's decision. I was thrown for a loop to say the least. I didn't have time to feel sorry for myself because I needed to defend myself up in Santa Clara County. So I accepted it, and continued to smile. I drove the 8 hours up the coast for my first hearing on this stupid ass case. I went to court and they continued the case for a month. I went back the second time, and they continued it again. The third time I appeared on this bullshit matter, I asked the prosecutor, Mr. Piazza, what he wanted. It seems that Mr. Piazza was a member of the tennis club that Robert was a member of. This was the first time that I experienced the humiliation of being out resourced. Hey, Robert was a buffoon, but he did have the connections in Santa Clara and had the money to buy whatever sort of justice he wanted. Piazza was from the same breed and he played it to the hilt. He said he would accept 30 days community service for a guilty plea. There was no way that I could perform 30 days of community service while living in San Diego. And there was also no way that I could move up to Northern

California for a month just to do that shit. And they knew it. But what they didn't know was that I wasn't afraid to do time in jail. This was some white collar bullshit and I wasn't down with it. So I asked Piazza if he had any other offer. He said, "The only other offer I have is 30 days in jail. Which I know you don't want to do." His eyes got as big as saucers when I said, "I'll take it." One thing that has always been a constant in my life, is that I have more time than money. Plus, I knew that in California, you never do your entire sentence. I would serve 18 to 20 days maximum. Piazza accepted my plea and I agreed to return two weeks later to surrender to authorities. I chose that time period, December 1, because I knew I would be home for Christmas. When I walked out of the courtroom, I looked over at Piazza and said, "Gratzie motherfucker." Appealing to the fact that his sell-out ass just fucked a fellow Italian. He didn't even look up. You ain't breaking me, as I smiled ear to ear.

I flew up to San Jose two weeks later and took a cab to the courthouse. I went in and when court resumed, they called my name. The judge asked if I was Ralph Edwin Richey, and I replied, "Yes." I showed the bailiff my driver's license and they took me into custody. I was taken to the local jailhouse and dressed out. We were then shackled and led to a bus. From there, we were driven to the Elmwood Correctional Facility. Hey, this was almost a resort type facility. It was clean, the lawns were like golf fairways, and the buildings looked like cottages. I was assigned to my building and I went in. This shit was like summer camp. There was only two problems for me. First, I chew Copenhagen tobacco to the tune of about a can a day. There was no chewing in this place, but you could smoke. I knew it would suck, but I would make it. The second problem was that I was from Southern California. See, in the Mexican prison population, there is a deep hatred between Serenos (Southern Californians) and Nortenos (Northern Californians). I was in Nortenos territory here and I would surly get "booked" if they discovered I was from the South side. Forget that I'm not Mexican, and that I'm not a gang banger, those idiots would have made an example of me if they found out where I was from. I stayed to myself and only spoke to those that spoke to me. I met a guy named Jaime, and he became my go to guy for cigarettes. I had been there for two days and I figured this would be an easy ride. Then one day I was watching T.V., and I got up to get some coffee. When I returned to the day room this bald-headed vato was sitting in my chair. I told him I was sitting there and he got up. He turned around and I began to sit down and this punk hit me with everything he had in the right ear. I didn't even spill my coffee, so when I turned around his eyes were like a deer in headlights. I put my coffee on the chair and faced him. I flat-blasted his ass in the chest and he fell against a chair. I began landing bombs on his face until it was a total mess. The only thing I remembered after that was being kicked in the head by what seemed like 50 homies. Apparently I was knocked unconscious and carried from the housing unit by deputies. I was taken to the hospital there on the grounds for a day. When I woke up, I had a headache but it wasn't serious. I was taken to the lock down unit inside the main jail. There would be no more cigarettes, but I would be much safer. In the lock down unit it was much more diverse. There was Black, White, Mexican, and Asian inmates housed there. I was much more comfortable there and I did my time by playing spades with the Black brothers and talking shit to the Mexican brothers that I bunked near. Actually, we had fun most of the time. The day I was called to roll-up, which means you are going home and to roll-up your bunk and all your belongings, I was overjoyed. I was going home to my family and we would spend Christmas together. As I waited by the door, this young homie named Jesus came up to me and hugged me. He said, "Rich, do me a favor homie, don't come back here. This shit ain't for you dude. Go back to SD and coach those kids like you're supposed to. I love you man." I said I would, and they popped the door. It wasn't until a long time later that I understood what Jesus was saying. Fuck, he knew I was from the south and he didn't tell anyone. Also, most of my time there I played spades and ate all of my meals with the Black brothers. That shit is a no-no, big time. To me it was just normal, but in that environment, you stay with your own...no questions asked. I exhaled deep and smiled.

I was released from Elmwood and looked for a pay phone. There wasn't one phone anywhere. I walked up to the counter and asked the woman where I could find a pay phone. She told me that there wasn't any on the grounds. What? I couldn't believe it. I asked her if there was a phone I could use to call a cab, and she said no. So I walked out the door and began my journey to find a phone. It was around 1:00 am. and pretty cold. I zipped up my jacket and hit the road. I had no idea where I was. I wasn't from here and since I had went straight from the courthouse to Elmwood on a bus, I was completely lost. I just walked towards the lights that were on the horizon. I walked in fields, jumping over fences and crossing freeways. Let me tell you, if you've never ran across a freeway at night, it's not a whole lot of fun! Damn, the cars roll up on you so fuckin fast. It's scary as hell. You had better have your running shoes on and that's no joke. After about 5 miles or so, I saw a city as I stood on a freeway overpass. I walked another mile, and I saw a Denny's restaurant sign. Yes! I practically sprinted to the Denny's. When I got there I was totally out of breath. I sat down on a bench and rested for a minute. I then got up and went to the pay phone. I called a cab company and they arrived soon after that. I rode to the airport feeling so happy. This shit was finally over. I went into the airport and purchased my ticket for a 7:00 am flight in the morning to San Diego. I slept in the airport until the morning came. I boarded the flight and when we took off, I looked out the window and said, "Bye San Jose, you'll never see my ass again!" And I meant that shit! I shook my head and smiled.

Since Mitz was working in San Diego and commuting down there from Escondido, we decided to move to Mira Mesa, Ca. after the first of the year. Shortly after we moved, two major events happened that would change the direction of my life. First, I got a job working as a counselor for a company called Circle of Friends. I really loved working with the young people there. It was a perfect fit. I was a counselor for level 12, at-risk young men. These kids had really been given a raw deal by life. Most of them came from dysfunctional families. Drug abuse, alcoholism, and parents that just plain didn't give a fuck. I related well with them because of where I was raised. Not that I experienced the kind of upbringing that they had. Hell, although we lived in the hood, we were Hood-Rich. Through my Dad's hard work, we had everything that I could ever want, including a swimming pool. But somehow I related with them and I understood their plight. They respected me because I was a high school coach and they couldn't run game on me. It was understood that if you respected me, I would respect you. Man, it seemed like I had found my niche in life. This was what I wanted to do for a living. The other major happening that occurred was Mitz found out she was pregnant. I continued working at Circle of Friends and life seemed to be going well. After working there for about 6 months, we were all called together for a staff meeting. At the meeting it was announced the company had decided that they would no longer retain any counselors that didn't have a college degree. Oh shit! This was me, and it really bummed me out. Man, Mitz was pregnant and I was out of a job. I had no choice but to keep my head up, keep smiling, and get ready for the birth of my son. We managed financially as we started talking about what we would name the newest addition to our family. It was 1998, and Mark McGwire and Sammy Sosa were challenging Roger Maris' single season home run record. The television coverage was incredible. I had started buying and selling baseball cards, and one day I noticed that Mark McGwire's birthday was October 1. It was mid-September and we agreed that if our child was born on that day, we would name him Mark. Sure enough, my baby decided to make his grand entrance on Oct. 1, 1998. He was a little angel! I really mean that, I'm not just saying that because he is mine. After a couple of weeks, I announced to Mitz that we were getting married. I know, I'm an idiot. She was fine with us just being common law, but I didn't want my son to be a bastard. So we called around and found a woman that would come to our home and marry us. Both of our parents, and brothers and sisters showed up on October 17, 1998 for our wedding. The woman arrived to marry us, and when I paid her, I looked at the receipt that she gave me. It read Sherry Smith. I recognized the signature, because it was the same as the one on my first marriage certificate. This was the same woman that married me and Julie in her home in Bonita. This can't be good I thought, but I didn't say anything. And like that, we were married. I had to smile.

Mark and I bonded from day one. Since Mitz worked during the day and I would attend baseball card shows at night, I would babysit him everyday. We had so much fun. I would feed him, bathe him, and get him dressed. We would stroll through the park in the morning and then return home for lunch. After feeding him, I would turn on the stereo and we would dance around. It never failed that if I played Blackstreet's "Before I Let You Go" he would go right to sleep. That became our song. This went on for 3 months and I noticed that Mitz really resented the relationship that Mark and I had developed. She started being real moody and hard to communicate with. One night, I was getting dressed to go to a card show and she walked into the bedroom and said, "Don't go tonight." I said, "I have to." She shouted, "Those fucking cards are more important to you than me." I was shocked by her outburst and said, "That's not true, but it's bringing in money. I won't be out very late, so just chill." She went downstairs and returned a few minutes later with a pair of scissors. She yelled, "This is what you're doing to me!" And began slicing her forearms over and over. The blood was pouring out of her veins, and I grabbed her and ripped the scissors from her hands. This was crazy! I calmed her down and agreed to stay home. Damn, this was becoming a pattern. If she didn't get her way she would either harm herself or threaten to harm herself. What the fuck was I going to do? I guess just keep smiling.

In January of 1999 we planned a visit to Mitz' parents house down in Calexico, Ca. located in the Imperial Valley. It is a little town that borders Mexicali, MX. Boy, I wish I never heard of that fuckin place, and you'll realize why shortly. But anyway, I had to attend a card show on that Saturday morning, so Mitz drove down there with Eddie (since I had him for the weekend), Michael, and Mark early in the morning. I went to the card show, and then drove my car to her parent's house. They were having a party that night and everyone was having a good time. I was just getting to know the family and trying my best to follow conversations that were in Spanish. I had never been in that situation before. See, I only speak English, period. Sure, I grew up in the hood and had many Mexican friends, but the only Spanish I knew was vulgar words. So trying to establish relationships with the family was very difficult. Mitz' brother asked me to go next door to a friends house to have some beers. I was 5 years sober at the time, but like a fool I went. We started drinking and having a good time. Later on, as he began getting faded, he looked at me and said, "I don't know if you know this, but don't expect to ever get close to me. I'm not close to my family and I won't be close to you." I turned towards him and said, "What the fuck is that supposed to mean?" He said, "Nothing, just don't ever expect me to accept you." Now I was kind of pissed. I looked him in the eye and said, "Motherfucker, where I'm from, you say some stupid shit like that, and you go out. I don't care if you ever accept me, I ain't lookin for your acceptance anyway. If you wanted to piss me off, you did. Now whatcha gonna do?" Like a punk he just turned away. Just about then, Mitz came over and saw me drinking. She told me to come home. I told her I would be in in a little while. She stomped off. I didn't want to leave things like that with her brother, so I stayed there and tried to straighten the shit out. Eventually, we agreed that it was just a misunderstanding, and things were cool. But he definitely knew not to fuck with me again. I walked back to her parent's house and the gate was locked. Her brother had left and I was outside the house, alone, and locked out. Luckily, I had my car keys so I just got in my car and went to sleep. Around 3:00 am I woke up freezing. I got out of my car and tried the gate again but it was still locked. I returned to my car and tried to get back to sleep, but it was cold as hell. I turned on the ignition and blasted the heater but it was just blowing cold air. I thought Fuck this, put the car in gear, and drove home to San Diego...toasty as a motherfucker. When I got home, I went immediately to bed. I'll deal with that crazy bitch tomorrow. I really wish that I had another choice, but I didn't, because it was freezing. The next day Mitz showed up with the kids and acted like nothing was wrong. I didn't talk to her. An hour after she arrived home, I saw my ex-wife Julie in the parking lot. What the hell was she doing here? I was supposed to meet her that night at 6:00 pm to drop off Eddie. Seems Mitz had called her in the morning and told her that I was drunk and stayed out all night. Julie was fired up, and there to pick up Eddie. I went up to Julie's car and she was livid. I told her the story and she seemed to understand. I agreed to let her take Eddie but I would pick him up from school, instead of at night, on my next visitation date. I went in the house and told Mitz that I was leaving for good. This shit had gotten too damn crazy for me and I couldn't stay with her anymore. She said, "Why didn't you come in the house last night?" I said, "Because the gate was locked asshole." She said, "I thought I unlocked it." I quipped, "No you didn't and I was freezing my ass off." She apologized and begged me to stay. I forgave her, but I never forgot the fact that she called my ex-wife. This bitch was dangerous! And yet I smiled.

I knew by this time that this relationship was bound for disaster but out of loyalty to my family, or more accurately, sheer laziness I stayed and tried to make it work. I couldn't go back to my parents house and I sure didn't want to face the humiliation of another failed relationship. It just seemed out of the question. I had already been divorced twice, had two sons (three if you count Michael) that I adored, and was married to someone that I thought I could help. I had long given up the idea that I would someday be rich, so I tried to focus on how I could be of use to others and society as a whole. I'm rough at times, but I really do care about people and I get a lot of satisfaction by helping others without regard to money. Money isn't important to me, people are. I'm secure in the fact that my heart is usually in the right place. I've never sought to hurt someone that didn't hurt me first. But I have to admit, I'm not a cheek turner, if someone disrespects me or seeks to harm me, hell yea they are going to get the same in return.

One day Mitz got a call from her Mom and she said there was an opening at the apartment complex that she managed in Calexico for an assistant manager. Mitz and I sat down and discussed the pro's and con's. The deciding factor was that we wouldn't have to pay any rent. Things were real tight for us because Mitz was the only one working. We had decided long ago that I would stay home with Mark. This move would provide us an opportunity to live a simple life. And at that point, I really wanted to go back to school, complete my degree, and possibly get a job like I had at Circle of Friends. So it was settled, we would move to Calexico on a trial basis for one year and then reassess the situation. We loaded up the truck like the Beverly Hillbillies and hit the road. This would be the beginning of my downfall. As I drove towards the desert I smiled.

We arrived in Calexico and moved in with Mitz' parents. Wow, it was total culture shock for me! It was like we were in Mexico, but we were still in the United States. Very few people spoke English and I really felt uncomfortable most of the time. I noticed that Mitz would often engage in conversations and completely forget I was there. I really began to resent it. She became someone that I didn't particularly care for. She was rude and obnoxious. And it got worse. I found out that in high school she was pretty much a bully. I knew she didn't have many friends and now I was learning why. It really tripped me out because except when she was wigging out, I had always felt sorry for her, because she was so weak and vulnerable. But things had definitely changed. She would get into actual fist fights on the street over a parking space. I could certainly understand her position because the folks in Calexico could be some of the rudest motherfuckers on the planet. Take this for example, one day I was waiting for a car to pull out of a space at the Post Office in Calexico. The car pulled out and drove off. As I began to pull in, this piece of shit truck with Mexicali plates, whipped around my left side and pulled into the space. Oh no you didn't bitch! I honked and honked, but this asshole just got out of the truck and started into the Post Office. I jumped out of my car, walked up to the fool, and said, "What the fuck are you doing bitch?" He turned around and said, "Que Onda?" I knew right then that this wasn't going to be settled verbally, so I looked down and saw that he was holding his keys. I grabbed them out of his hands and threw them on the roof of the Post Office. I just looked at him and said, "Buenos Dias Nigga" and I got back in my car and drove off. I couldn't believe that shit! It was definitely not my finest hour, but I kind of felt good about it. In between laughing my ass off, I smiled. These people, especially the folks that came across the border from Mexicali, could be some of the rudest motherfuckers that you've ever seen. If you were standing in line at the grocery store, old ladies would just cut in front of you like you weren't even there. And the worst part of it was that I knew they saw me. They would look away like it wasn't shit. I said on more than one occasion, "Excuse me bitch, where you going?" They would pretend to ignore me but I would just box them out like I was waiting for a rebound. It was crazy! So I understood why Mitz would get frustrated, but I couldn't have her brawling in the streets. That was another strange thing about Calexico. People there would take an ass-kickin in an effort to appear tough. Where I'm from, if you got your ass kicked you were a punk and/or an idiot. False bravado was the norm in Calexico. I've always believed it was more important to be tough than to act tough. That means showing respect to get respect. See, I grew up with guys like Kevin Mitchell. Yes, he of the New York Mets, San Diego Padres, San Francisco Giants, etc. fame. Kevin was one bad dude. Not bad in the sense that he was a bully, but bad in that he was big, tough, and could fight like Smokin Joe Frazier. I think Darryl Strawberry learned that shit first hand when they were members of the Mets. Well anyway, even though me and Mitch were the same age at 16, he would play hoop with the men at the Mt. Miguel gym on the glass court while I played with the dudes that were our age on the side courts. On the times that I was fortunate to play on glass with Mitch, if he kicked the ball out of bounds and said it was his ball...Shit, it was his ball! No questions asked. That is how I grew up, if you could kick my ass, you were right. There were no moral victories in my neighborhood. Period. But down in Calexico, these fools would front like they were tough, and when someone would put them in check they claimed some ignorant pride by taking a beat down. Fuck that! And another thing surprised me, these fools carried knives. What was this shit? The Outsiders! Please! The G's in my neighborhood carried guns. If you carried a knife on my block you better be a whittling motherfucker! So as you can see, things were just different here than what I was used to. I vowed to adapt, conquer, and smile.

After we were there for 3 months, Mitz learned she was pregnant again. She had never started the job at the apartments because of some bullshit. I soon learned that this was just normal Calexico procedure. She was on complete bed rest because the pregnancy was very difficult. Probably from throwing down in the streets like an animal. Mitz' father came home one night and said they were hiring at his job. It was at United States Gypsum where they made Sheetrock. I applied the following day and was hired. I went to work there stacking Sheetrock and learning the ropes on a new line that they were starting up. We needed money so there was no time to think about about my bad neck or any other physical problems that I had. Imperial Valley has the highest unemployment rate in the country. So you can't be picky. This place was a living hell. It was 130 degrees inside and I carried that Sheetrock for 10 to 12 hours every day. But hey, I had a job, and that was more than most people could say down here. On July

22, 2000, Mitz went into labor. I drove her to the hospital and she was checked in. I called work and they gave me the day off. But since my team at work was having a barbeque that evening, they asked if I could drop off the tortillas and the radishes that I had promised to contribute. The doctor came in at about 2:00 pm and said that Mitz probably wouldn't deliver until late in the evening. I decided to take the stuff to work and then come back. I drove to the dirt area next to the plant, and saw some of my guys sitting under a tree. I got out of my van and dropped off the stuff. They all congratulated me and I drove off. This get together was on a farm, so as I drove out I didn't notice that it was moist land. It just looked like dry dirt to me. Well I got stuck in the mud, and I mean stuck! The van wouldn't go anywhere. I got out and walked over to the guys. They were laughing and were clowning me. I sat down and they said don't worry. The guy that owned the land, Ramirez, was getting off work at the plant in an hour or so. He had a tractor and would pull me out. So we sat there and had a few beers. An hour and a half later, someone said that Ramirez was on his way. I went to the van and rolled the windows down because it was hot as hell. As I got out of the van, a Sheriff's car rolled up. The kid Sheriff walked through the mud and asked what was going on. I told him that I stopped by to drop off some stuff for our barbeque and got stuck in the mud. He checked out the van and turned to me and asked, "Have you been drinking?" I replied, "Yes, but not until after I got stuck." I explained that the guy Ramirez was coming with a tractor and he was going to pull me out. After that, my father-in-law was on his way, after getting off work, and he would drive us both home. The Sheriff then said, " Turn around. " I said, "For what?" He said, "Just turn around." I said, "Not until you tell me why. I'm on private property, I wasn't driving. You need to give me a reason why." He grabbed for my left hand and I cold-cocked him with an overhand right. He was face down in the mud! Oh shit, what have I done? Any contact I had ever had with authorities to that point, no matter how much bullshit it was, I always complied completely. I just stood there in shock. Within a minute, 2 CHP cars rolled in like the Dukes of Hazzard. They jumped out and took me down at gunpoint. They snatched me up and loaded me into their car. They drove me down to the interstate on-ramp where they met a Sheriffs vehicle. They pulled me out of their car and slammed me in the Sheriff's car. The deputy drove me to the Imperial County Jail. When I got there, the receiving deputies were laughing. They processed me and put me in a holding cell. I sat in there wondering, "What the hell have I done?" I fell asleep until morning, and a woman deputy came in. She said, "Are you ready to go home slugger?" I was out of it. I whispered, "Yea." She sat down next to me and said, "Hey, don't worry about that shit last night. That kid is an asshole and I'm pretty sure he deserved it. We've been laughing at his stupid ass all night." I didn't say anything, because I didn't fully know what she was talking about, but I pretended that I did. They released me and I walked home feeling like a total dirt bag. When I got home, my mother-in-law met me in the driveway. I said, "How's Mitz?" She said, "Well, you have a new son." I took a shower and we drove to the hospital. There was my precious boy Bobby. Named after my best friend Robert. As I held him, I felt so unworthy. I just held him close and repeated, "I'm sorry for not being here honey, I'm so sorry for not being here." That night I explained to Mitz what had happened and we took Bobby home. On a brighter note, when I went to court they dropped the Assault on a Police Officer charge and agreed to accept a Wet Reckless charge. I agreed and paid a fine. Thank you God! I looked up and smiled.

So I worked at USG for another 5 months, and one day the stacker machine just stopped. The wallboard was stuck and I jerked it out. I fell on my back and it felt like I broke my back. Both of my legs were numb and I couldn't move. They loaded me on a golf cart and drove me out to the main office. When I got there they gave me two Tylenol and told me to rest. A half hour later, some fat son of a bitch came in and said, "Are you ready to go back?" I said, "No." I couldn't even stand up. He said, "Do you need some more Tylenol?" I said, "No thanks." I told him to either take me to the hospital or I would call an ambulance. A guy from Human Resources came in and said, "Let's go, I'm going to take you to the hospital." He said it like I was really putting him out, so I got pissed off. In spite of the pain, I got up and walked to his car. We drove to this little clinic in Brawley and walked in. They laid me on a table and, what I thought was a doctor, came in. He started feeling around and suddenly cracked my back. He was a fuckin chiropractor and he just adjusted me without as much as an x-ray. I yelled in pain and told them not to fuckin touch me again. Damn, that shit hurt! I called Mitz to come get me and she did. Needless to say, I sued USG and never returned. But that's how it is down there. People are so hard up for jobs that if you have one, the employers treat you like shit, and no one says anything for fear of being fired. Not me! I came from a civilized part of California and knew my rights as an employee. I received my settlement and now I was a free agent. Now what? Well first, I will smile.

I don't remember how, but I found out that Holtville High School was in need of a Junior Varsity baseball coach. I met with their athletic director and was appointed to the position that day. Yeah! I was so happy, maybe things were going to go my way for a while at least. I've never had to think about teaching the game of baseball. There were a few great men in my life like Jerry Puerile Sr. and Ed Olsen that taught me the fundamentals of the game at a young age. I know the game like the back of my hand. I once heard a man say that, "I've spent my whole life gripping a baseball, and after further review, I realize that it was the other way around." And that was my experience. There is a passion for the game that runs so deep that you can never give it up. Well, I went right to work with the youngsters at Holtville High. They were good kids and they put forth their best effort each and every day. I became close with some of their parents, including a man named Bill, who was the father of one of my pitchers named Billy. Billy was a huge kid even though he was still growing. The problem was that Billy didn't throw very hard. He was an intimidating figure on the mound, standing around 6 foot 4 inches. But his fastball just didn't have the zip to drive hitters off the plate. When I was in college, I was a pitcher and stood 5 foot 10 inches, and weighed around 170 lbs. But my fastball was in the low 90's. So Bill and I would often discuss how to strengthen Billy's huge body so he could bring the heat. Actually, I think it bothered Bill more than it did Billy. Billy was a great kid and just had fun playing the game. Well, I did all I could, but Billy was still growing, and he ended up having a decent season. He just didn't blow opponents away. But throughout the season me and Bill had a good friendship. He was a judge in the youth drug court. I would also keep tabs on my player's performance in the classroom. If they were slipping, I would let them know that they had to pick it up or they would be dismissed from the team. I had a kid named Woodie that didn't have much talent, but he loved the game and worked hard to improve. He lived with his grandparents and I guess he would often be disrespectful to them. I had given my cell phone number to all of my players because I was a walk-on coach, and not on campus during the day, I expected them to call me if they weren't going to make it to practice. Also, before the season, I had a meeting with their parents. I also gave them my cell number to call me if they were having any trouble at home. Well Woodie's grandmother would often call and say, "Coach, Woodie won't listen to a damn thing I tell him and he's running his mouth like a sailor around here. Would you please talk to him? I said, "Sure, put him on the phone." Woodie would get on the phone and I would start by saying, "Woodrow, is it true that you are disrespecting your grandparents?" He would answer, "No, that bitch is lying!" I told him, "The fact that you would call your dear old grandmother a bitch tells me that you're lying and I'm ashamed of you kid! Listen, you better go tell her you're a piece of shit and you're sorry. If you don't, I promise I will run your fat ass so much tomorrow that you will puke everything that you've ate for the past two days!" Choked up, he would say, "Alright Coach, I'm sorry." Then his grandmother would take the phone back and say, "Thanks again Coach, you're the best. God bless you." I would say, "God bless you."

So as you can see, I had some characters at Holtville High, and although it didn't show in our won-loss record, we were better at the end of the season than we were in the beginning. And we had a lot of fun. Every team that I've ever coached, I made it a point to have a lot of fun. I believe that as a coach, I will never diminish a kid's love for the game because of some egotistical trip of mine. At the end of the season we had a team party at Bill's house and I gave each player a piece of major league memorabilia that I had in stock. It was a great time and we parted with the feeling that our season was a success. I was proud of the job I had done, and I smiled.

I began looking for a way to occupy my time, so I noticed an add in the newspaper for applicants for the Imperial County Civil Grand Jury. I went to the courthouse and applied. They had a drawing to choose members that night and I was selected. Wow, I was a member of the 2005-2006 Grand Jury. I really didn't know what it entailed, but I had come to the conclusion that I needed to learn the court system because I seemed to be on the wrong side somehow. I went into it with a passion. I raised my hand when they said they needed a Law Enforcement Committee Director and they gave it to me. It gave me the opportunity to tour all local Police Stations, the Imperial County Jail, etc. with just a phone call. But quickly I realized that the phone calls were the key, because it gave these facilities time to get their act together before I came. It was a joke! These places were so phony and I knew it. But I also discovered that there wasn't anything we could do. So the whole thing was glossy as hell. I did my year of service and didn't re-up for the next term. It was a great experience and something to add to my resume. Plus, I was still smiling, and that's a good thing.

When I started serving on the Grand Jury, I decided to contact the varsity football coach at Calexico High School. His name was Joe Apodaca and we met one afternoon. We got along real well. When he learned that I had coached at Oceanside High School, one of the best high school programs in San Diego if not in the state, he hired me as his Receiver's and Defensive Back's coach. I'll never forget the first day of practice. Since it got so hot down in the Imperial Valley, we started the first day of hell week at 6:00 am in the morning. They ran the sprinklers all night and the field was drenched. Here I was in shorts and ankle socks and the mosquitoes were eating my ass alive. I pretended that it didn't bother me, but I'll tell you that I showed up for the afternoon practice smelling like Off, head to toe. And in the afternoon, I couldn't believe these folks were still practicing. I was running my station while we put the players through drills and I was blowing my whistle as usual. It suddenly dawned on me that I was feeling woozy and about to fall out. I toughed it out but I knew this shit was different from what I was used to. Hell, if the temperature reached 102 degrees in San Diego, practice was canceled! Here, it was 112 degrees in the shade and these fools would just press on like it wasn't shit. We had some decent athletes, which was nice after coaching at Holtville High. I got to know some of the kids and learned that some of them played J.V. baseball the previous year. The problem was that they were seniors now. No wonder we got our ass kicked at Holtville when we played Calexico. These chumps had juniors playing J.V when I had an all freshman squad. Ain't that some bullshit? We laughed about it on many occasions. I loved those kids. They took me in and also accepted my sons Mark and Robert like little brothers. That was really important to me because my son Eddie would often tell his little brothers how he would kick it with the likes of Junior Seau at Oceanside High, who was currently starring for the San Diego Chargers. And that would really get under Mark's skin because, without a doubt, Mark was the best athlete out of my sons. That shit burned him up! He loved Junior and he couldn't figure out why Eddie got to grow up around Junior and here he was in fuckin Calexico. But like I say, my players in Calexico, treated both Mark and Robert like little brothers. I had a tailback by the name of Ernie Sanchez. That kid had so much talent. We spent a weekend in San Diego at a passing league tournament at USD, who were coached by Jim Harbaugh. Ernie made such a good impression on Jim's staff that Bill Arnsbarger, legendary NFL coach, pulled him aside and inquired as to where he was going to college. Ernie had no clue, he just played. My coaching associate, Alfie Silva, and I pulled him aside and asked him, "Do you know who that is?" Ernie said, "The old guy?" We said, "Yeah motherfucker, that's Bill Arnsbarger, he's a legend in the NFL!" Ernie shrugged and responded, "Cool." Damn, he had no idea! Oh well,

Ernie was great and he had a little brother named Oscar. Oscar, who was a Oakland Raider fan (I'm a Charger fan), would take Mark and Robert aside and fill their heads with anti-Charger bullshit. He was great with them. I would often show up to practice and jump his ass for telling my boys that the Raiders were the shit. Man, we had so much fun...my entire family. Ernie and Oscar didn't continue their football careers after high school but they became U.S. Marines and are the ones that people speak of when they talk about brave young men that protect this great nation. That's something that I must mention, I've been so blessed in my 25 year coaching career, to lead the best young people this country has to offer. I'm not boasting, hell, I'm humbled to have had the opportunity. If you went around and saw what these kids are doing with their lives, I'm sure you would be impressed. But anyway, at Calexico, we ended up the season 3-8. But once again, we had fun. On to the next adventure. Smiling, always smiling.

Right before the end of the season, Mark came to me one day. He had tears in his eyes and he said, "Dad, I have to tell you something. There's a kid at school that pounds me every day." I said, " What do you mean he pounds you?" He said, "He punches me all over, everyday." I told him to go to bed and I would take care of it the following day. I called the Principle at his elementary school, Grace, and I explained the situation. She said she would contact the other kid's parents and see if they could come in that day. Grace called me an hour later and said we could meet at 11:00 am later that day. When I walked into the office, I heard a man talking in her office. He was saying things like, "Well we can't be raising sissies, the world is a tough place, and kids need to learn to be tough." I listened for a minute or so while this asshole ran his mouth. Fuck this shit, homeboy better be ready to face my worst. I walked into Grace's office and looked at this big mouthed, piece of shit farm worker. I asked Grace if this was the father of the kid that was bullying Mark. She saw the look in my eyes and nodded yes. I had just left the gym and was pumped. I turned towards the guy and stuck my finger about a half inch from his nose and said, "So you're a tough guy huh motherfucker? Well my name is Coach Richey from Calexico High and if your son ever touches my son again, I'll break you in half. How the fuck are you going to sit in here and go on and on about being tough, when I know you're about to piss yourself right now? Either you teach your kid to respect others and keep his hands to himself or I will. You may run that shit down on your wife and kids at home, but let me tell you something punk, I'm from a little town called fuck a wet-back up and you're making me homesick! Either heed my words or get fucked up fool!" And I walked out of the office, while Grace shouted, "Mr. Richey I'll call you!" I just yelled back, "O.K." Neither Mark nor Robert ever had a problem at school after that. Not just because of this incident, but because I became friends with the head custodian, Chris De La Rosa, and all the rest of the school's personnel. Chris watched over them during school hours and he would tell me if there was any problems. I couldn't help but to smile.

From that point on, I drove Mark and Robert to school and picked them up after school. No matter what! It became such an enjoyable part of my day to walk down to the school and wait for them by this big maple tree. They would come running to me and we would walk home while they shared how their day went. I was determined to not let the ignorance of that place infect my son's spirit. I made the decision to move down to this hell hole, but I would damned if my boys would suffer because of it.

After the football season at Calexico High the Athletic Director, John Moreno, asked me if I would be interested in taking over the Head Baseball coaching position at the high school. I told him I would definitely accept if they offered me the job. About a week later, John called and offered me the position. I accepted as promised. He told me to go over to the Personnel Office and fill out the necessary paper work. I had never been to the Personnel Office, which was a little trailer located in the high school parking lot. When I was hired as an assistant football coach, I was sent to the District Office, filled out the paper work, and sent to the high school. That was it. So I just figured this was how it was done for a head coaching position. I filled out the endless forms at the Personnel Office and they sent me to get a TB test, a drug screening, and a background check. I went and did that and returned to the Personnel Office. They said they would contact me within a couple of days. I was overjoyed! I had longed to be a head coach and now it was coming to pass. I waited for a week and nothing happened. I called the Personnel Office and they said that my background check had come back negative and they were withdrawing their offer to become the baseball coach. What? This bullshit from my past was now preventing me from doing what I loved to do, what I was good at, and what I needed to do to support my family. And it was the start of a heartbreaking process that would follow me for a long time. I went down to the Personnel Office and attempted to explain my past but no one seemed to be interested in hearing it. I finally asked if they had my check for coaching football. They said that they were unaware that I was employed by the school and that I wasn't going to be paid anything. What the fuck?! I had just spent three months coaching both the varsity and junior varsity football teams, and they weren't going to pay me my measly stipend that I was promised? Hell no! I did exactly what the high school told me to do, which was go to the District Office and fill out the paper work. After I did that, they told me I was good to go and sent me to the school to do what I do. After a lengthy battle with every idiot employed by the Calexico Union School District I finally received my stipend. But I was out of a good opportunity with the baseball job. I couldn't help but feel this shit was racial. I had got to know a lot of people around town and I knew that a lot of them had real serious convictions on their record. I wasn't Mexican and they were screwing me because of it. I knew it and they knew it. And it really hurt me because I was lucky enough to be raised in a diverse cultural environment and always stood for equality. To tell you the truth, I was hurt, angry, devastated, frustrated, and offended. Everyone at the school like John Moreno and Joe Apodaca were dumbfounded. I told them that I appreciated all their support, but no way would I return to the school the following football season. They understood and we remain friends to this day. But as far as the racist morons at the school district, fuck them assholes! I sulked for about a week and then I picked my ass up and pressed on. Smiling, always smiling.

Mitz got transferred to another apartment complex in Calexico so we moved the following weekend. My dad and my brother came down and helped me move. It was about 111 degrees outside and we busted our ass all day moving. When we were done we were beat. I went to the store with my brother and he bought beer. Even though I hadn't drank any alcohol for over a year, I made the decision to have a beer with him. One led to two and before I knew it we had both polished off a six pack apiece. We went back to the store and got another 12-pack and promptly finished that one. My dad and brother left and I was sitting in the living room. I had a twelve pack in me and for some reason I decided that I needed to go for a drive. I drove to El Centro and just cruised around. As I was leaving the city I was stunned to see the police car lights behind me. Oh shit! That is the worst feeling in the world when you know you're up to no good. My heart sank as I pulled over. After a chat with the officer, it looked like he was going to let me go. Then he called his partner over and asked, "Do you smell alcohol in this car?" His partner stuck his head in my window, took a sniff, and said, "Yep, it does." They took me out of the car and gave me a sobriety test. I'm pretty sure I failed because they arrested my ass. They drove me to the jail and booked me. I sat in the cell and wondered how I could be so stupid. In the morning they released me and I made the hideous "Walk of Shame" back to my house. How could I be so ignorant? I was a fucking fool! This had become a nightmare. I decided right then that I was done, and I vowed to go to any length to quit drinking for good. And it worked...for a long while, but not for good. I was down, but not out, and I smiled.

I sat down one day and wrote an in-depth moral inventory of my life and faced some depressing facts about myself. First, I had to change. I couldn't keep putting myself in vulnerable positions by making bad decisions. I couldn't take one step forward and two steps back. I had to get off my ass and make things happen. Like the old saying, Procrastination or masturbation, either way you're fucking yourself. But I had to be realistic. My driver's license was suspended so I had to find something that I could do that was either home-based or close to home. Since there was nothing close to home, my option was clear. I started searching for home-based business opportunities. Now this was an adventure in itself. There are so many bullshit hustlers out there that it's really comical to see what some people call a business. But after wading through the con artists, I found a real possibility. It was doing Judgment Recovery. Basically, you find potential clients at the records department at the Superior Court that have been awarded a monetary judgment in small claims court. You then contact them and find out if they have ever recovered their settlement. If not, you offer to collect it for 50% of whatever you do collect by filing liens, wage garnishments, etc. Hey, half of something is better than all of nothing, right? I ordered the package and began studying the material. After a week I was ready to go. I obtained a business license and I began Desert Judgment Recovery. I would spend hours at the courthouse searching records for prospective clients. I would also kill two birds with one stone on some days when I had to appear for my DUI case. My business was doing fairly well and I enjoyed it. But it became apparent that I wasn't going to make it down in the Valley because a lot of potential clients and debtors spoke only Spanish. This made it impossible to track down debtors or communicate a contract with clients. So I cleared up all of my client's cases and I began searching for my new goal. Smiling, always smiling.

In the back of my mind, I knew what I wanted to do. It was obvious what I was good at and what I enjoyed. I wanted to work as a counselor and coach young people. What was also obvious, was that I needed to go back to school and obtain my degree to achieve my goals. But first I needed a job. One day I decided that maybe I could make a living as a long haul truck driver. I went to our local employment office and got information on job training. I found out that there was a Class A Commercial driving course beginning soon in El Centro. I enrolled and began training a week later. I completed the course and obtained my Commercial Driver's License. But when I searched for employment, I found out that no one would hire me because of my driving record. Seems insurance companies are not willing to cover drivers with two alcohol related convictions on their record. I should have researched this endeavor more before I began it, but I had a new experience. So I pressed on. Smiling, always smiling. The only local college in the Imperial Valley is Imperial Valley College. Otherwise known as IVC. The only thing I knew about IVC was that it was a brutal place to play baseball. When I was in college I used to dread making the trip down there. First of all, they sucked and I knew we would spank them. We had a very good team which eventually won the Pacific Coast Conference title. Next, it was hot as hell. And finally, the wind would blow so hard out to right field that the games usually became a joke. But if I was going to go back to school, I figured I should become familiar with the place. I also figured that I could coach while going to school. It was probably just wishful thinking but I believe in dreaming...and dreaming big. I drove to the college one Tuesday afternoon and watched the baseball team practice. After it was over, I approached the head coach and introduced myself. His name was Jim Mecate and I knew right away that he was a guy I could work with. Jim is a devote Mormon and a man that carried himself with extreme dignity. He doesn't swear, drink, use tobacco products, etc. He reminded me of Dave Barrett at Oceanside High. We chatted for a while and I finally got up the nerve to ask him if he could use any help on his coaching staff. He thought for a moment and said, "We can't pay you much, but I'd love to have you here." I replied, "That's great because I don't need a lot." And with that, I became the newest assistant baseball coach at IVC. I was worried about a background check, but in college, they just present you before the Board of Governors, and they accept or deny you. I was accepted and I went to work. From day one, me and Jim became good friends. Since he was also the Athletic Director and a teacher, I would help him out around campus during the day. Jim and I are total opposites except for one thing, we both like to laugh. I would try to tone down my expletives around him but he definitely appreciated my sense of humor. That would certainly come in handy given the lack of talent in the Valley. One thing that hadn't changed from my days in college...IVC sucked! Most of the players hadn't been taught the fundamentals of the game. Jim had played at BYU and I had played at Grossmont and we were fortunate enough to have learned the proper way to play the game. Our kids at IVC had survived on pure talent (which wasn't much) and now they were going to be going up against some of the best players in California. They needed help and we were responsible to provide it. We did the best we could, but the fact is, our guys were simply over matched once conference play began. But as always, we made the game fun. We would have so much fun on road trips by clowning around with the kids. Never in a hurtful way, but we would all rag each other. In fact, I finally got the team together and announced, "If you can't take a joke, you're not allowed to ride in our (with me and Jim) van on road trips. Be honest with yourselves, if you get offended easily, you're going to have to ride with Coach Lechuga (another assistant coach)." So it was settled, we had our Goon Squad, and the rest of the players rode in the other van. We had so much fun and we laughed ourselves sore. By the time the season was over, our guys could rag opposing players like professionals. It was great. The following winter, Jim and I were talking one day about goals. I told him that I would like to return to school and get my degree. I told him about my desire to be a counselor and a coach. He said, "Why don't you enroll here?" I said, "I can't afford it." He answered, "Apply for financial aid." I said, "I won't be eligible." He shot back, "How do you know? It can't hurt to apply." So I applied for financial aid ...And I got it! Wow! I was going back to school! I enrolled, and after a little trepidation about being in class with much younger people, I began attending college again. It was kind of strange being in class with my players, but for the most part, I had a blast. I would work on class projects with my players like David Corona and Benny Carter. I would do the same with others like Patsy Landeros and Allyson Rodriguez. I could go on for days naming these young folks, like Matt Rojas (who was on the basketball team), who helped make me feel so comfortable, but let's move on. It was just a great environment and I was having so much fun. The teachers were great, the kids were wonderful, and the coaching staff in the athletic department were excellent. I made true friends and I couldn't have been happier. I was really busy with going to school full-time, working part-time on campus, and coaching baseball year round. As part of my job at the school, Jim made me the announcer at all home basketball games. I really enjoyed doing that. The best part of the job was that I got summers off. I would take Mark and Robert with me to IVC during the summer to swim, play basketball, take batting practice, play volleyball, etc. One summer, my friend Andrew Robinson (the men's assistant basketball coach) was holding a summer basketball camp for youngsters. I asked if I could help out and he said sure. I brought Mark and Robert along with me to participate. The local newspaper sent photographers to cover the event. The following day, I opened the newspaper to the sports section, and on the front page was a huge picture of Robert trying to dribble the basketball through his legs. When I showed it to him his eyes just lit up. He was so excited. I mean it's cool the first time you see your name in the paper, but Bobby was staring at a half page picture of himself. Wow! So needless to say, my family and I became a fixture on campus at all sporting events and anything else going on at the college.

Unfortunately, Mitz had become jealous of the time I spent at the school. She started accusing me of cheating with the students on campus. Was she out of her mind? I was an old man to these youngsters and it was simply ridiculous. But she would lose her mind if one of the girls at school would say, "Hi Coach." It was just plain stupid. The fact of the matter was that after 3 years at IVC my 13 year marriage to Mitz was in shambles, I was due to receive my degrees with honors in Alcohol & Drug Studies, Behavioral Science, Social Studies, Physical Education, and Human Relations. I was determined to go back to San Diego, and I was going to fight for custody of Mark and Robert. One of my professors told me one time, "Coach, IVC is an excellent place to study but don't expect to get a job down here, there's nothing my friend." I knew this to be true and I had decided that I would move back to San Diego after graduation and seek employment in the counseling field. Things had gotten so bad at home, that Mitz and I knew we were on our last leg. Her outbursts were becoming so regular and violent that I wanted to get the boys out of there as soon as possible. My studies revealed to me that she was suffering from a severe personality disorder and she refused treatment. But she wasn't going to go down without a fight. I hated living in our home and she was making it impossible to get along with her. I wasn't much better though. I resented her so much for what she had done to us in the past that I really just stopped trying. I would spend most nights down at the computer room in our apartment complex chatting with friends on facebook and myspace. Some nights I wouldn't come into the house until 5:00 am. This just fueled her accusations that I was cheating more. At that point I had been sober for 5 ½ years, and I was ready for a change. Although our trial one-year in Calexico had turned into 10 of the worst years of my life, I did feel sad about leaving IVC. I pondered this fact as I was putting the gear away on the baseball field. We were in our last week of practice in winter league. It was December 6, 2009 and I was depressed. I sat down on the bench and reviewed my last 3 years at the school, my relationships that I was fortunate to have, the kids that played for us, how they truly accepted me like no one in Calexico had, the great days I spent in class, etc. A tear fell from my eye as I just sat. Not just from sorrow but also because I had injured my knee the previous week while racing my players. We were running sprints and on the 6$^{th}$ or 7$^{th}$ one, I felt a sharp pain and heard a pop in my left knee. I figured I would have it checked out after school let out in a couple weeks. Right then I remembered that I had two beers in the trunk of my car from a friend's party over the weekend. They were 24 oz. Bud Lights. No I couldn't do it. Not now, I had come too far. I walked to my car which was parked right behind the dugout and opened the trunk. There they were. In a move that I'll regret for the rest of my life, I dug them out and took them over to the bench. I cracked them open in record time and guzzled both. That wasn't half bad, I thought. I put the gear away and locked up the field. I started my car and rolled out to the highway. The baseball field was located just west of the main entrance to the campus. So you just had to pull out onto the highway for about 300 yards and into the main entrance. As I waited to turn left into the school, I revved my engine. When it was clear, I pulled into the entrance. Right then some idiot shot in front of me and I slammed on my brakes. My foot slipped off the brake and I gunned the gas. My car hopped a curb and got stuck in a planter. I was stuck. Oh shit! I had hit a light pole and was fucking stuck. The air bags had deployed and there was smoke everywhere. I got out of the car and looked around. A campus police officer came running up and said, "Are you alright coach? I already called the ambulance and the police." I thought, No motherfucker, No! Sure enough, a Sheriff car rolled up right then. He asked if I was alright and I told him yes. He asked if I had been drinking and I told him no. He told me to sit down on the curb. Just then Jim came running from the gym. He asked if I was alright and I told him yes. The officer came over and asked me to blow into this pipe-like device. I did and he went back to his vehicle. He then called Jim over and they were talking. When they finished, the deputy came over to me and said, "Coach, you're over the limit, you're being arrested for DUI. I'll need you to step over to that Highway Patrol vehicle behind you and get into the front seat. We aren't going to handcuff you and embarrass you." I thanked him and did what I was told. Jim came over to the car and said, "I'll pick you up right now." I gave him a wave and we took off. We arrived at the California Highway Patrol office. We went inside and sat down. The Patrolman asked if I wanted any coffee and I declined. Man, my life was over. All that I had worked for was shot to hell. Fuck! Just then, Jim walked in. I signed some papers and we left. We talked on the way to my house and he came in and talked to Mitz when we arrived. This was the end of life as I knew it. Jim left and I took a shower and went to bed. There was absolutely nothing funny about this, but I smiled, what choice did I have?

For the next three days I didn't do anything but lay around the house, drink, worry, and stress. The more I tried to find some hope to go on, it seemed like reality would step in and crush it. I began to realize that if this was considered my third DUI, I was facing mandatory jail time. I stressed over that fact and drank as much as I could get my hands on to mask the fear. I once heard the acronym for fear is Fuck Everything And Run, and I was running my ass off! I certainly didn't want to face the facts. The facts were my marriage was over, I didn't have a car, I didn't have a driver's license, I probably had no chance of getting a job, I didn't have any chance of getting custody of Mark and Robert, and I had no way to get the hell out of Calexico. I was at my breaking point. I'm a person that swears a lot but one thing I never do is take the Lord's name in vain. I never damn God in any way. On this day, I had a total spiritual break down. I sat in bed and cursed God for allowing me to ruin my life and for just leaving me hanging. Was it the truth? Of course not. But this self-pity party was in full swing. My knee hurt real bad and I was sore all over. I decided to take a bath. I ran the water and got into the tub. As I sat there shaving my head, I decided that I had had enough. I took the disposable razor and broke it. I removed the razor blade and looked at my arms. I wasn't going to pussyfoot this shit like Mitz, I was going to take my life. I sliced the big vein at the bend of my right arm. The blood flowed like a hose. As the tub filled with blood I sliced my leg where my knee hurt. I passed out, and the next thing I remember, I was riding in the back of an ambulance. They took me to the hospital where they stitched me up and gave me some Ativan. I stayed there until morning and then they transported me to the Behavioral Health unit in El Centro. When I arrived, the only people on duty were two guys from my class at school that were interning there. They said, "What's up coach?" and I gave them some bullshit answer. They asked me if I wanted to stay or leave. I told them that I wanted to leave, so they discharged me immediately. Mitz was pissed! She saw this as an opportunity to win custody of the boys since she had such an extensive history of mental illness. So I was discharged and we went home. I apologized to the boys and promised I would never do anything like that again. It was tough, but I managed to give them a smile.

The next day, Mitz took the boys and moved over to her parents house about two miles away. She would come over to the apartment complex and screw around with her scumbag friends and return to her parent's house in the afternoon. It was totally stupid because she and the boys would sleep on the floor there, when they had their own beds at home. And she was protecting them from me? What an idiot! I came to the conclusion that I had to rectify this situation as soon as possible because she would do anything to win this thing, no matter how much it hurt the kids. It was all about Mitz and her revenge. We began talking on the phone and whenever I would mention leaving Mexican Mayberry, she would lose it. I urged her to bring the boys home because they didn't deserve to be uprooted simply because it was over between us. She refused. On New Year's Eve day she called and said that she was going to take Mark and Robert to Mexicali, Mexico, and I would never see them again. I said, "If you do, I will kill your ass!" Big mistake on my part. What I didn't know was that she was at the Calexico Police Department and had me on speaker phone. Hey, I learned from previous mistakes that you never say anything threatening on a recording device. This was 2009 and the Calexico Police Department seemed to think it was a good idea to entrap someone in their home. Mitz was in full on destruction mode. She figured if she couldn't have me, she would destroy me. Any one that knows me, knows that if you want to hit me where I live, just go after my kids. Nothing is as important as my sons, period! We spoke for another 45 minutes and I apologized to her for saying that I would kill her and she apologized for threatening to take my sons to Mexico. We agreed to meet at the apartment office at 7:00 pm to discuss this mess. At 6:55, she phoned and said she was at the office. I went down the stairs and started across the lawn to the office when I heard some rustling behind the building and 8 cops jumped out from behind the bushes. They were pointing shot guns at me and yelling, "Get down, get down!" I was dumbfounded, but I got the fuck down. If I had seen this coming, in the mental state I was in at the time, they would have carried all of us out of that complex in body bags. The Spring Valley in me knows that to be a fact! Because at that point, my dislike for firearms had all but disappeared. And the thought of ending all of this chaos made me smile.

The cops hooked me up and stuffed me in one of the cars. They drove me to the Calexico Police Department and led me into a room. This little detective came strolling into the room like he owned the joint. They sat me in a chair and left me cuffed. The kid detective leaned against a desk and faced me. He began all buddy buddy like. I'm thinking here comes some good cop, bad cop bullshit. He said, "Mr. Richey, I hear you're a coach at IVC and a real nice guy." I responded, "I'd like to think so." I still had tobacco in my mouth and he pushed a metal trashcan in front of me so I could spit in it. I inquired, "Detective, what's this all about?" He said, "It's about threatening to kill your wife." I said, "I just said that in response to her threatening to take my children to Mexico, and saying I would never see them again. Isn't that a felony?" He said, "Only if she does it. Mr. Richey we have you on tape, so denying that you said it isn't going to fly." I put two and two together and said, "So you entrapped me, right? Because she called me." He said, "That's for a judge to decide. Right now you're being charged with a Felony Threat and Arson." I shouted, "Arson, what's that shit about?" See, two nights prior to this, someone broke into Mitz' office and started a fire. The office had been broken into a half dozen times in the past 6 months. On the night of the fire, I was awakened by the fire alarm at 2:30 am. I phoned Mitz over at her parent's house and told her that the alarm was going off. Then I went back to sleep. That was it. The little sawed off detective leaned in and said, almost begging, "C'mon, just admit that you did it." I shouted, "Fuck you bitch! If you try to railroad me on this shit I will sue your punk ass." Immediately, he grabbed the trashcan and put it up to my face and told me to spit my dip out. So I spit my dip out on the hand he was holding the trashcan with. He goes off, like a he's a big shot on Hill Street Blues, saying, "Get this son of a bitch out of here." The only problem was that the only people in the room were him and me. I looked around and starting laughing. He turned around and said, "You know, you're not a very nice guy." I said, "That's the best you got Pedro?" He says, "I'm going to love seeing you in that orange jumpsuit." And I said, "Fuck you, you little pint-sized Fez lookin motherfucker!" So with that, they took me to the Imperial County Jail. They charged me with a Felony Threat, but not the Arson. Because I didn't do it. Since I knew the truth, I simply smiled.

I get to the jail and they sit me down and start reading me my charges. As I mentioned, they charged me with the Felony Threat, which also carries a strike. In California we have the three strikes law. That means if you get convicted of three felonies, you are sentenced to life in prison. I couldn't believe this shit. I got booked, processed, and sent to the housing unit outside the main jail called Campo. I entered the unit and went to a bunk in the back. Obviously, this wasn't my first rodeo, so I knew procedures. I put my hygiene bag in the bunk drawer. I then went to get a drink of water. As I was sipping the water from the fountain, I noticed this punk (out of the corner of my eye) pulling my hygiene bag out of the bunk drawer that I had placed it in. The bag has stuff like a comb, toothpaste, soap, etc. I went back to the bunk and opened the drawer, and sure enough the bag was gone. At that point I knew I wouldn't be housed here for long. It was almost time for the nightly count, so I just waited. When the CO's came into the unit and yelled, "Count", I rushed over to stand by the vato that jacked my shit. When the CO walked by, I turned to the dude and said, "Yo, enjoy that bag bitch." And I cracked his punk ass with a left hook right on the button. He went right out! The badges rushed over and took me down. Then they hustled me out of the unit. See, you can never get punked, even one time in jail. If you do, it'll never stop. And the reason why I waited for the CO's is because if I would have done that to the dude with no badges around, his homies would have booked (kicked my ass) me. I was transferred to the main jail. I went to the newbie cell in G unit. I sat on my bunk and thought how this had to be one of the worst fuckin days of my life. But I calmed myself with the thought that this shit would be over soon. Boy was I wrong! This deal was just getting started and it would get worse before it got better. But since I didn't know that, I smiled.

I woke up the next day wondering where the hell I was. I sat in my cell trying to put this thing together in my head. It was New Year's Day 2010. This certainly wasn't the first New Year's Day that I woke up not knowing where I was. The only difference was that it smelled like piss and there wouldn't be any college football today. I realized that I would be there for at least 4 days because today was a holiday, then the weekend, and there is no court on Mondays. The soonest that I would go to court would be Tuesday. When my cell door popped open I took my paper thin mattress out to the day room and laid it on the metal table. Then I tied my sheet on to it to act as a mattress cover. I took it back to my cell and placed it back on the rack. I went out to the day room and sat on a bench. Eventually, a guy named Buck came over to me and said, "You're Coach Richey from IVC, huh?" I said, "Yea, who are you?" He told me that his name was Buck and he was Cliff's brother. Cliff Benson was an excellent player for me at IVC. We shook hands and he gave me the rundown of the unit. The father and son above me were Memo and Don Willie, they were in for murder. The guy next to me was named Fish, he was the javedo (the key) he kind of ran the unit. Across the way were three brothers named Javier, Rudolpho, and Raymundo. They owned several fitness clubs in the Imperial Valley. I had read about them in the local paper. Buck told me that the guy down at the end had went to court the previous day and was sentenced to a 6 month diversion program for stabbing his girlfriend in the neck three times. I felt for this guy's girlfriend, but this was great news. I would surly be out of here on Tuesday. I just chilled until Tuesday came, and on that day I woke up early and was ready to go. They came at 5:30 am and took us one by one to be shackled. Then we were led single file down a long hallway to the holding cell inside the jail. Inside the holding cell we were crammed in like a puzzle with bodies laying everywhere. The cell was no larger than 12 x 12 and we had at least 25 dudes in there. About 5 hours later, an attorney banged on the door and yelled, "Richey." I jumped up and went to the door. The public pretender had the CO open the door and let me out. He looked over the case file and said, "You should be out of here today. You don't look like you belong here anyway." I said, "I don't." They called my case and I sat down at the defendants table. The judge scanned the case and said, "There's nothing here." I was thinking to myself, "Great, I have to go home, find some boxes, pack my stuff up, and get the hell out of Calexico. Just then a bailiff stepped up to the judge and whispered something in his ear. The judge listened, and then said, "The victim is here, and we're going to have a hearing right now." Oh shit! And hell no I wasn't smiling!

After a few moments the door opens up and here comes Mitz shuffling down the aisle looking like a Mexican Phyllis Diller. She was tore up from the floor up. She looked like she just got hit by a truck. Nicely played you fuckin bitch! She slowly walked up to the bench and slowly sat down by the judge. I'm thinking, "Really?" as she sat there with her head down and trembling like a leaf. If this shit was happening to someone else it would have been comical. But it was happening to me, so not so much. Like my Dad says, "The difference between a recession and a depression is, a recession is when my neighbor is out of work, a depression is when I'm out of work." This circus was at my expense so I was flabbergasted. The hearing began and my attorney asked Mitz, "Are you afraid of something?" She nodded yes. He asked, "Of what?" She pointed at me. He said, "Are you telling me that with Mr. Richey sitting here shackled from head to toe and 8 armed deputies in the courtroom, you're afraid?" Mitz nodded again, never looking up. The judge asked her a few questions and she just morbidly nodded back. The judge looked up and announced, "There is sufficient evidence here to hold Mr. Richey over for trial. Next case." What the fuck?! Like Chris Rock says, "I've seen better actin in tough actin Tinactin." The deputies led me back to the holding cell. I stayed there until court was over. Some guys were elated, and some guys were like me with that deer in the headlights look. I heard some dudes telling of how they got caught with two handguns in their trunk and their sentence was a fine and the cops would keep the guns. He would be released that day. I couldn't believe it! We were on our way back to G unit and a deputy Garcia looks over at me and says, "Richey, your wife is one evil bitch. I saw her a minute ago laughing with her sister in the hallway. They were carrying on and saying it was a great performance. Slapping high fives and shit. I sure wouldn't want her karma." He eventually gave a statement to my attorney, but as you'll see later, it didn't make a damn bit of difference. But at the time, with my faith in the justice system still strong, I smiled.

My next court date was set for a week later. I got back to G unit and went to my cell. I heard a dude outside say, "Who's the whiteboy?" I was pissed off, so I figured I would regulate this shit right now. I've always hated the word whiteboy. First of all, because I'm not and secondly because at 50 years of age, I'm certainly not a boy. Not to mention the word whiteboy is used as a put down and said by most races to demean you. At the very least it's degrading. If anyone tries to deny this fact, they are a bitch in my book. So I walked out of my cell and saw this disgusting, wanna-be gangster named David running his mouth. This kid was straight wrecked. He had his shirt off and looked like a pregnant chimp with his drug scares all over him. He had a shaved head and a braided goatee. He was popping off like he was running shit. I walked up to him and said, "You make it a habit to call people you don't know names like whiteboy? I'm close to 50 years old, and I damn sure ain't no boy motherfucker. Don't ever refer to me as a whiteboy, Nigga. Would you like it if I called you brownboy, bitch?" That clown was stunned. I don't think that wanna-be vato had ever heard a white man talk like that. That fool had a body that looked like a tube sock filled with yogurt, so I knew that I would bust his ass if anything jumped off. I finished with, "Listen, if I hear your big ass mouth while I'm taking a nap, I'm going to get up and drop a 5th floor brick on your fat ass, understand?" And that was that, I never heard the term whiteboy again. After a few moments, Fish walked by and said, "Tell that youngster what he needs to hear Coach." I nodded and laid down for a nap.

I think it's only fair and accurate to tell you now that in no way am I some gangster, OG, bad ass, or hard guy...especially at my age. But I can fight and will fight if I deem it necessary. It was essential to learn to fight in my neighborhood. But I've never been one to go picking fights. Although I grew up with folks of all racial lines red, yellow, black, white, and brown...the worst ass-kicking that I ever got was a by a white kid named Ronnie Grudel in 6th grade. It had to be the worst ass-whoopin in Rancho Elementary history. Ronnie looked like a Gump with his bald head, black hard soled shoes, green Toughskins, pointy teeth, and flannel long-sleeved shirt (even though it was 95 degrees outside). One day he was playing kickball and kicked the ball over the fence with his hard-ass shoes, and it hit me in the back. I walked over to him and said, "Who kicked the ball?" Ronnie said, " I did Eddie, I'm sorry." Damn, I wish I knew then what I know now (how to accept an apology, especially when there is no intentional harm done)...But no, my stupid and immature ass walked over to him and smacked him like a bitch. That fuckin jackal kicked me in the shin with those hard-ass Thom McCann shoes so hard I thought he broke my leg. He then jumped up towards my neck and bit a chunk out with his pointy ass teeth. And finished it off with a knee to my nuts. Man, I was done, unfortunately he wasn't. That fool picked up a metal lid from one of those Snack-Pack pudding cups and started swinging it like a kung-fu master. I was up against a fence and he sliced my left index finger so deep that I thought he cut it off. I still have a half inch scare on that finger. So I was there with blood flowing like a river from my neck and my finger, my nuts were half way up my bung hole, and I was just sure that my leg was broken. He stepped back and said, "You give up?" I said, "I gave up when you kicked me with those combat boots." He just walked away. The lesson learned here was never fuck with a foster home kid...no matter what he looks like.

So here I was, in jail, laying in my cot after waking up from a nap. I was depressed and couldn't believe that my life had gone so wrong. How could I have let my beautiful sons down like this? The despair that I felt was almost overwhelming. Just then, Memo Regelado walked into my cell and said, "Hey Coach, how you doing?" I said, "Not too well bro." He sat on the stool next to my cot and said, "I know things look bad right now, but God has a plan for you and it will be great. We have Bible study every night up in Rudolfo Mascarena's cell at 7 o'clock. You're welcome to come. Do you speak Spanish?" I answered, "No." He continued, "That's OK, we'll get one of the other brothers to translate. Do you have a Bible?" I said, "No." He pulled out a pocket-sized version of the New Testament and gave it to me. He said, "We're reading Romans right now so just start there." I said, "Thank you, I'll be there." He said, "You know, we are all paying the price for our sinful nature, so Romans is a good place to understand it and learn to combat it. Would you like me to pray for you Coach?" I said, "Sure." We both knelt next the cot, and Memo said the most beautiful prayer that I've ever heard. When he finished, we both stood up and he gave me a hug. He looked me in the eye and said, "I'll see you tonight, read Romans, and we'll discuss it tonight." He left and I looked at the Bible. Man, this young man was facing life for murder and he was peaceful and willing to share that peace with me. I wanted what he had. I opened the Bible to the book of Romans and began reading. When I was done, I meditated on it, and I hit my knees. I said the following prayer that I had learned in A.A. "Father, I offer myself to thee, to build with me, and to do with me as thou wilt. Relieve me of the bondage of self, that I may be of use to you and to others. Take away my difficulties, that victory over them, may bare witness of thy love, thy power, and thy way of life. Amen." I stood up and felt this incredible peace flow through me. I wasn't happy to be there, but somehow I knew that things would eventually be OK. I sat at the little table in my cell and continued to read. As I read, I got a feeling that I needed to write. I walked around the unit and asked guys if I could borrow some paper and a pencil. A guy named Jose gave me some paper and his cellmate, Drew, gave me a pencil. I thanked them and returned to my cell. I sat down and searched that little Bible for verses that pertained to hope, strength, and courage. When I came across a verse that spoke to me, I wrote it down along with it's address. I continued doing that for the rest of the day, non-stop. When it was 7:00 pm I heard someone yelling, "Iglesia, iglesia, iglesia!" I looked out my cell door and guys were walking upstairs to Rudolfo's cell. I stepped out of the cell and looked at the clock on the wall. It was 7 o'clock. I grabbed my Bible and rushed upstairs. The tiny cell was packed. As I squeezed in, Memo announced, "Hey guys, this is Coach." Everyone greeted me warmly, kind of like an A.A. Meeting.

A kid named Juan came over to me and said, "Coach, do you need me to translate?" I said, "Yes, if you would." We jumped up on the top rack of the bunk and settled in. Everyone started clapping and singing in Spanish, "This is the day, this is the day that the Lord has made, that the Lord has made. I will rejoice, I will rejoice and be glad in it, and be glad in it." When the song was over, Rudolfo Mascarena read from the book of Romans. Guys raised their hands, one by one, and gave their thoughts on what the scripture meant to them. Juan translated what they were saying since everyone spoke Spanish. After about 45 minutes, Rudolfo asked me, "Coach, would you like to share?" I said, "First of all, thank you for inviting me here tonight, I really needed it. I look forward to joining you guys every night. Today, God put Memo in my path to show me the way to Him, and He has placed you guys in my life to learn to praise Him and understand His word. Thanks again." Memo said, "Felix goes to court tomorrow, so let's pray for him." Felix walked to the middle of the cell and knelt down. Everyone gathered around him and Javier, Rudolfo's brother, said a prayer for him. When it was over we all walked out of the cell. Every one of the guys that was there came up to me and hugged me. They made me feel so welcome. I got to know their names and where their cells were. Most said, "If you need anything Coach, just ask." I went back to my cell and laid down on my cot. I didn't understand it at the time, but I felt true joy for the first time in my life. It's easy to feel content when everything is calm and serene in your life. But when everything is going crazy around you, and you're not...Man, it's incredible! I read a little of my Bible and then prayed, saying, "Father, I know you have a plan for my life. You promise me in Jeremiah 29:11 that this is so. I thank you for your love and protection in my time of need. I know that you are here and you will never leave me. Please place a hedge of protection around Mark and Robert. I know that there are forces of evil at work in my life and I ask for your protection from their flaming darts. Please soften Mitz' heart and lead me out of this place in Your time, not mine. In Jesus' precious name, Amen." And even though it felt like I was sleeping on solid metal, I slept like a baby. With a smile. For the next week my day consisted of reading my Bible, jotting down scripture, praying, eating chow, taking a shower, and going to Bible study. If I wasn't doing any of those things, I was doing push-ups and talking to the guys in the unit. The night before my court date, all the brothers gathered around me while I knelt down, and they said a prayer for me. The next morning I awoke with such hope. Today this would finally come to an end. I was sure of it. After being shackled we began the walk to the holding cell. But instead of waiting 5 hours for court to begin, this time it was only 2 hours. Why? Because this time we weren't going to jail court, but to the Superior Courthouse. They loaded about 8 of us into what was essentially a dog catcher's vehicle. It was like we were mangy mutts on the way to the pound. When we reached the courthouse, they had us exit the vehicle and stand in line outside the rear of the courthouse. It felt so good standing there in the sun. I hadn't felt the sun or sniffed fresh air in over a week. It didn't last though, because they led us up some stairs and into this metal box. We all sat in there for 4 hours until court began. When it did, they began calling names. Guys would go out, face the judge, and come back. Through our conversations in the box, I knew what each guy was charged with when he left. All agreed, after hearing my story, that I would be out of jail that day. I sure hoped so. I had good reason to be hopeful. Every dude that came back to the box was happy. One guy who had hit his neighbor with a rock, in the face, was going home with just a fine and 10 days community service. Another guy that was facing 7 felony counts was being released with a fine for beating up his aunt and was arrested with methamphetamine and weed in his possession. So I was sure that I would be released today with a fine at the most. When my name was called they took me out of the box and led me into the courtroom. I stood next to my attorney as they called my case. I listened intently to hear what the prosecutor's offer was. But he didn't offer shit! He just said that he would like to continue the case for another week while he prepared further. My attorney said, "Don't worry, we'll just waive time now, and they will drop all charges next week." I didn't like it but I agreed. So it was settled, we would waive time and come back the following week. The gavel went boom and that was that. I went back to the box, and while everyone celebrated on the way back to jail, I just prayed. This was just a bump in the road, so I smiled.

If you're wondering why I didn't call anyone to bail me out, that's simple. In this age of cell phones, I didn't know anyone's number by heart. Who does these days? Since I didn't have my cell phone, I had no one to call. Memo and the other brothers offered me the use of their calling cards, but I simply didn't know anyone's phone number. And anyway, my bail was set at $50,000, and I would never ask anyone to pony up $5,000 that I couldn't pay back any time soon. Also, Mitz was telling my Dad and other members of my family that I had lost my damn mind. That I had got drunk, burned down the office, lost her custody of Michael (her ex-husband had sued her for custody in

November because she was just cruel to him and he wanted to live with his Dad), traumatized our sons with a suicide attempt that had landed me in a mental hospital, that I had drunkenly demolished my car and got another DUI, was fired from my job, and had gotten arrested for a felony threat because I threatened her at gunpoint. As you can see, between the facts and the bullshit that she threw in, it sounded like I just went off the deep end. Since no one ever came to visit me, I figured this was the case. As far as my friends go, let me say right now, I have the best friends that any man could ever hope to have. The support network that I have been blessed with is second to none, but I had no way to contact any of them. And Mitz sure as hell wasn't going to let them know that I needed help. But that has always been the case with me. I keep my problems to myself and just struggle through with a joke and a smile. It's foolish pride, I know, but it's also why I've never lost a true friend. My friendships run deep and have stood the test of time. Period.

So I was back on my cot in jail, wondering when this nightmare would be over. Through the grace of God, I had trained my mind to not worry over the kids, or even think about them, since there was nothing I could do while I was locked up. I focused on the day I was released and how I would deal with it then. It's amazing what you can cope with if you mix determination and prayer. I continued to study the word of God and attend Bible study. I began going to jail church on Sunday mornings and attending a recovery program offered by Volunteer's of America. The VOA wasn't up and running outside anymore because 4 months prior, I read in the paper, two idiots that were undergoing treatment had stole the VOA van and committed armed robbery in El Centro. The instructor for the program told us that they were doing some remodeling, but I knew the truth. The state had cut funding and the program was terminated. I knew this because some of my classmates at IVC were doing their practicum there and had to find a new one after the debacle. Yes, some churches and recovery programs are full of shit too. Don't kid yourself! But I wanted the court to know that I wasn't sitting on my ass while I was there and kept on getting involved with anything that was productive and positive.

I met with my public pretender, Brian, and he assured me that on my next court date the prosecutor would offer me a plea deal. Well, when we went to court, I had no such luck. They just continued it again. For the next month and a half, the same shit would happen. I would get up at 5:00 am, go through the shackling, get in the dog catcher mobile, go to the courthouse, wait in the box, go in front of the judge, and they would continue it. About the third week, I received a restraining order in my cell, and a detective called me out of the unit. I went to the window and he said, "That is a restraining order. You are not to contact your wife or Mark and Robert Richey in any way. Do you understand?" I said, "Sure, thanks." Two days later I had to appear at a hearing for the restraining order. I went to court in the morning for the threat, it was continued, and I was driven back to the jail and returned to my cell. About 30 minutes later, I was called to go back to court for the restraining order. So I pulled my jumpsuit back on and rode to the courthouse for the second time that day. My attorney Brian told me not to say anything because it could affect my criminal case negatively. I went into the hearing and sat at the table. Mitz had hustled the assistance of some women's advocacy group and they just beat me to shit. I looked over and saw Mitz' scumbag brother and I winked at him. I had met some guys in the unit that told me what a punk he was in high school. As I was instructed, I didn't say anything. It killed me because I could understand the protection order for Mitz, but for my boys? That was ridiculous! Hell, the judge on the bench knew me to be a great father. His name was Poly, and Bill had introduced me to him at a game one time while I was there with Mark and Robert. From then on, Poly would often say, "Hey Coach", when I would see him. And of course, Mark and Robert would always be with me. But I just sat there and Poly approved the protection order for a year. I can't see or talk to my sons for a year? You have to be kidding me! Man, Brian better know what the fuck he is doing!

I had been in jail for 2 months and I was tired of being fucked with. I met with Brian before my 8th appearance, and I told him in no uncertain terms, "If the other side offers you anything that will get me out of jail, you take it! I don't care if it's a felony, if they give me a strike, if I'm put on 3 years formal probation, anything. If I can get out, I'll sign it. I'm not getting lost in here, do you understand?" He nodded, and went into the court. He returned about 45 minutes later and said, "They're offering a deal if you plead to the Felony Criminal Threat, take a strike, serve 3 years formal probation, and pay a fine of $1,500." I said, "Where do I sign?" Brian said, "Mr. Richey, just give me a little more time, and you won't regret it." I looked at him, shook my head, and said, "Time? Listen to me, I've spent 2 months in that shit hole and the only thing that I've gotten from you is empty promises. You go home at night, I go back to a fuckin cell. I can care less about the strike, I'm not a criminal, I won't get another one. I don't want to have a felony on my record, but I will if it gets me out of here today. By the way, if I sign when will I be released?" He looked down and said, "Immediately." I said, "Then tell them I'll sign." He shook his head, got up, and went out the door. I was ready to do flips, I was so happy. I was getting out of that dungeon, finally! Brian returned with the paperwork and I just initialed each one because I was so anxious to be done with it. I went into the courtroom and told the judge that yes I had agreed to what was stipulated and he accepted it. Done. Brian reached over to shake my hand, and I walked away. Finally, it was my turn to rejoice in the box! It was my turn to say, "It'll be OK." to someone that just got royally screwed by the court. I took my final ride in the dog catcher mobile back to the jail. When I got back to my cell I began packing the few items that I had obtained in the last 2 months. Like my written scriptures, my Bible, and a couple of books. I rolled up my mattress and I was ready to go. I went upstairs to Memo's cell and told him the good news. He, and his father Don Willie, were genuinely happy for me. We hugged and I thanked him. He said, "Coach, don't leave Jesus here. I've seen it happen so many times, guys come here and accept Christ, then when their name is called they throw everything in the trash and bolt out of here. You're a good man and you have a lot to offer the people out there. Keep Him with you." I said, "I definitely will bro." Right then, there was some yelling downstairs, and I heard a loud thump. We rushed to the door, and I couldn't believe what I was seeing. Jose and Drew, who were friends and cellmates, were fighting. They were throwing down in the middle of the unit. Everyone came running and before I knew it, the Paisas and the Surenos (two rival Mexican gangs) were in an all out war. It turned into a bloodbath. Guys stabbing each other, kicking each other, throwing anything they could get their hands on, etc. It seemed like it went on for hours, but it probably only lasted 15 minutes or so. It's amazing how much physical harm can be done in just a few minutes. Memo, Don Willie, and I stood in shock while we overlooked this grotesque scene. Finally, the CO's busted in and began pepper spraying dudes, tackling them, and clubbing them. It took a while but they had everyone locked down in any cell they could find, including us. I sat there with Memo and his Dad and the whole unit was dead silent. I heard over the loud speaker, "Richey, roll up." Yes! The words that I had waited to hear for the past 2 months. I banged on the door and yelled, "I'm in here, 206, I'm in here. Upper 206, I'm in here." A CO came to the door and said, "Richey?" I said, "Yes." He opened the cell door, I said bye to Memo and Don Willie, and I walked out. I couldn't believe how much blood was on the floor. A CO said, "Watch your step, it's slippery in some places." I walked over puddles of blood, I walked through puddles of blood, and I walked around puddles of blood. It was like something out of a horror movie. When I was almost to the door, I heard guys yelling, "Later Coach, take care brother, take it easy Coach, be good Coach." I turned around and yelled, "Stay up fellas, see you on the outside!" The CO's opened the door and I walked out. I was brought to a room and they gave me a canvas bag with all of the clothes that I was arrested in. It felt so good to put on my own clothes and especially my shoes. I had worn these oversized deck shoes for two months, so my Nike Airs felt like pillows on my feet. When I was dressed I was sent to a window, where I signed for my belongings, and then led to a door. Over a loudspeaker, I heard an officer say, "Just push the door." I did and it opened. I walked out, and I was free. I was outside. The sun, the breeze, fresh air...I was free. I closed my eyes and said, "Lord, please go before me and guide my path." And I started walking down the road, with a big ass smile on my face!

As I walked down the road, I thanked Jesus for his grace and mercy. While in jail I came to the conclusion that my spiritual journey had been really screwed up in the past. I always believed in God, but I had a problem with Jesus. In my experience, most Christians were phony and hypocrites. They would throw their hands in the air and stomp around like idiots on Sundays, but by Tuesday they were the biggest sinners I knew. I wasn't down with the charismatic stuff. It just wasn't me. I had no problem using the term God as my higher power to speak of the source of my strength and inspiration while in A.A. But when people would throw Jesus into the mix, I kind of cringed. I believed in the old saying that religion is for people who are afraid to go to hell, but spirituality was for people who had already been there. It worked for a while, but now I was up against a wall, and I needed the true power of my Lord and Savior Jesus Christ. I now had a relationship with the one true living God. With that in mind, I decided to go see my friend Danny in Calexico. He was friends with me and Mitz, but we were pretty tight, along with his wife Sandra. I was walking down the road looking like the Hitchhiker when a truck pulled to a stop and the driver asked if I wanted a ride. I accepted, and I jumped in the passenger side. He didn't speak English and I didn't speak Spanish so we just rode for a minute. He looked over and said, "Calexico?" I replied, "Si." That was it for my Spanish. I hoped he wouldn't say anything else, and he didn't. See, I had learned a while ago to always answer Spanish speakers in English because then they would know that I don't speak Spanish. In the past, if I answered in Spanish, folks would start spitting Spanish at me and I would be lost. So it was just easier to answer in English and save myself the embarrassment of having to say, "No habla espanol." And them answer, "Oh." I don't know why I answered the driver in Spanish, but no worries, guess he wasn't a big talker and that was fine with me. As we reached Calexico, he stopped at a stop sign and I said, "Aqui." And he pulled over. I jumped out and said, "Gracias." and he said, "De Nada." Alright, so I do some Spanish but not enough to carry on a conversation, so I just don't fuck with it. I walked to Danny and Sandra's house and they weren't home. I sat with my paper bag full of scriptures and my Bible on a chair in their front yard. I really hoped that they would let me stay with them while I regrouped and got my shit in order. It felt good to sit in the sun and let my eyes adjust. When I was in jail, we were only allowed one hour per week outside in the yard. That much time indoors really does a number on your eyesight. So I sat there for about 2 hours, and finally Danny and Sandra drove up. Sandra was driving, so Danny got out of the passenger side. I walked up to him and he hugged me. Sandra came around and hugged me too. We all went in the house and I told them what really went down the night I was arrested. Sandra told me that Mitz was fired by the apartment complex for causing all the commotion there, including blaming me for the fire in her office. I bet that bitch didn't expect that, but any sane individual would have. She went on to tell me that all of my belongings were in a storage room at the complex. Sandra knew because she also worked at the complex as Mitz' supervisor. Danny asked me if I wanted to go with them to their church to pack up some food bags for the needy. I said, "Sure." We went over to the church and packed the bags. Danny had sent someone to get Jack in the Box hamburgers, so when the guy returned, Danny offered me a Jumbo Jack. I took that burger and ate it in no time flat. Damn, that was the best burger I ever had in my life! Shortly after that, a church service began. Danny told me to wait in the lobby because the service was going to be in Spanish. I told him, "No, Dan, I've attended church in Spanish for the last 2 months. I'm cool." So I went in and listened to the message as best I could. When it was over we all drank coffee outside. I hadn't gotten around to asking Danny if I could stay with them, but I wouldn't have to, because he walked up and said, "Hey Ed, Sandra's brother works for the Salvation Army and he has a place for you to stay." I said, "Where is it?" He answered, "In El Centro." Since I really didn't have a choice, I told him, "Cool." But of course it wasn't. I got into the car with Sandra and she drove me over to the apartment complex to pick up some of my stuff. My heart sank when we pulled into the complex. This was the first time I had been here since the night of my arrest. I thought of the good times with the boys there. I felt like crying but I held it in. We went to the storage room and she unlocked it. I went in and looked around. Where was my stuff?! There were only 2 3 x 3 boxes in the corner and 3 locking trunks that I kept my baseball cards in. What the fuck?! Hell, I had tons of clothes, at least 30 pairs of shoes (probably 10 that were still in their original boxes, yes, I'm a shoe whore), baseball equipment, picture albums, etc. None of it was here. What the fuck had she done with my stuff? I was furious! As I was looking around in disbelief, Sandra said, "Just pack a bag of your clothes and you can get the rest later." I figured she was in a hurry, so I just grabbed a big Mizuno sports bag and pulled as much of my clothes from the boxes as I could, and stuffed them into it. We left the complex, picked up Danny, and drove to the Salvation Army in El Centro. When we got there, me and Danny walked up to this door, and he banged on it. It was pitch black and the place was kind of spooky. Someone from inside said, "Who is it?" I almost expected Danny to say something like, "The eagle has landed or the fat man walks alone." But he didn't, he said, "It's Danny, Sandra's husband." This guy opened the door and asked Danny, "Is he sober?" Danny answered, "Yes, he's sober." The guy said, "No drugs?" Danny goes, ""No." I was standing there like a fuckin moron and these dudes are talking about me like I'm retarded. The guy opened the door and let me in. I stepped into this hallway and Danny stuck his head in the door and said, "He's Coach Richey from IVC, he's a good guy." And the guy slammed the door shut. Dude wasn't impressed in the slightest. He showed me to this little room where there were bunk beds lined all around it. There was only him and a guy named Fred there. I introduced myself to Fred and he seemed to be a real nice guy. As for the other dude, I had him pegged right off as a con man and an asshole. It didn't take long for him to prove me right. On the way there Danny bought me a can of Copenhagen tobacco and I couldn't wait to have a dip. I hadn't had one for 2 months, and I felt the itch like a heroin addict. I got situated by hanging my clothes up in this closet, putting my underwear and socks in a drawer, and picking out a bed. I went into the hallway and put in the fattest dip I ever had and I got undressed to take a shower. After showering I looked on this table that had food on it. I went and asked the asshole if I could get something to eat. He said, "Do what you want dude." So I did. After eating a bowl of cereal, I laid on the bed. Damn, it was nice. I had slept on that cold metal cot for the last 2 months, without a pillow, no blanket, and a mattress that could have been confused for a parachute. This bed had an actual mattress and a pillow. I asked Fred if they had a San Diego phone book. He searched around for a few moments, and then came back with one. I flipped through the pages and found my Dad's listing. I asked Fred if there was a phone. He gave me his cell phone and said, "It's all yours buddy." I thanked him and dialed my Dad's number. It rang a few times and then my Dad answered, "Hello." I almost started crying, but I choked it back and said, "Hey Dad, it's me Eddie." He was real cold and he said, "What do you want?" I said, "Nothing, I just wanted you to know that I'm out of jail and staying at the Salvation Army in El Centro." He said, "Well I guess that's what you get for treating your family the way you did. I wouldn't of done a one-eyed dog like you did your family." I said, "Dad, you don't know what really happened. If you'll let me explain..." He cut me off and said, "You don't have an explanation. I don't know why on God's green earth you would do somebody like that, but I guess it just is what it is." I said, "Dad I need help." He grumbled, "I don't know what you're going to do, because you're not coming here." I said, "Dad I don't have anywhere to go, I'm staying in a shelter, and I'm on probation. I don't think I can leave even if you said I could stay with you." He said, "Well, you better find somewhere to stay." And he hung up. I tried calling back, but he didn't answer. That bitch had turned my own Dad against me! I could just imagine what she was doing to Mark and Robert. I went over to my bed and prayed. When I was done sending up my knee mail, I climbed into my bed, and with tears in my eyes...I smiled.

The following morning I woke up and Fred was having coffee. He asked if I wanted some and I said, "Sure." He poured me a cup and we drank coffee and watched the morning news on T.V. He said we needed to get dressed and go over to the Salvation Army store. We got over to the store and this lady came out and introduced herself as Helen and she told me to get a shovel and go to the back of the store and pick up all the trash. When I turned the corner and saw the pile of trash she was talking about I said, "Shit". This entire parking lot was filled with trash 2 feet deep. I got to work and shoveled that trash into the trash bins until I had blisters on both hands. After 3 hours of that, Fred came and got me and said we needed to go to Brawley where another store was located. We drove over there and I unloaded boxes of junk for 7 hours. Trying to separate the good stuff from the junk was pretty difficult because in my humble opinion, this shit was all junk. When I was done we closed up the shop and went to a house to pick up some more junk. I guess this woman had a yard sale that day and the junk she didn't sell, she was donating to the Salvation Army. As we got out of the truck it began to rain. In the pouring rain, Fred and I loaded up everything that she had, which was a bunch of stuff. No wonder no one bought this trash because it was just that...trash. While we were driving back, Fred looked over at me and said, "We're probably going to get in trouble because we're only supposed to pick up the stuff that we can re-sell. But since it was raining, I didn't want to go through it all, so that's why I just said load it all." I said, "Fred, let's find a Dumpster and unload it. Then we'll say that there was nothing that was worth anything. What do you think?" Fred thought about it for a moment and said, "Screw it, I'm sure it's all good." I said, "Cool." When we arrived at the El Centro location we parked the truck and went inside to eat. This was kind of cool, being able to choose from a refrigerator what we wanted to eat. Not that it was gourmet or anything, but they did have lunch meat and cheese, some left over chicken, and plenty of sweets. While we were eating, a man with one arm came in and told Fred to come into the hallway. Fred went in to the hallway and the one arm dude just ripped him a new asshole. He was calling him every name in the book. Fred came back into the room and said, "See, I told you I was going to get in trouble. The stuff we picked up was total junk." Fred was such a nice guy and I really felt sorry for him. I told him not to worry about it. The next day we went to the Brawley store and had a pretty good day. Before we closed up, Fred told me to pick out some church clothes for the following day. I asked where the church was, and Fred told me it was at the El Centro store. It was then that I learned that the Salvation Army was a Christian organization, and they held their own services. I looked through the clothes and since nothing fit, I went back and told Fred that I would just wear my own clothes. He said, "Do you have slacks, a dress shirt, a tie, and church shoes?" I said, "No, but I have nice khaki's and a nice polo shirt." Fred said, "No, you have to wear dress clothes." I said, "Nothing fits." He said, "Well Ed, just find something, you gotta." I looked through the clothes again and I picked out some black high-water slacks, a long-sleeved white shirt with a butterfly collar, a checkered red and black tie, and some black shoes that were scuffed so badly that they looked brown. The following morning I put on the outfit and looked like a total clown. The sleeves on the shirt were about three inches too short and I only had white socks. I looked like Michael Jackson and Pee-Wee Herman's love child. Before we got in the van to go over to the store, the asshole that greeted me the night I arrived came over, and said, "Do you have any money?" I said, "No." He then gave me three pennies and said, "Here's something to put in the offering plate so you can receive the blessings too." I took the pennies and put them in my pocket. We went to the store and I attended the service. I even put the pennies into the offering plate...let the blessings begin! When the service ended we were to have a holiday dinner. I got in line to get a plate and Fred told me to that we weren't included. Me and the other three guys that were staying in the home were stationed behind the serving table, and we served everyone in the congregation. Then we were told to clean everything up and go back to the house. We cleaned it all up and returned to the house. When we got there, I couldn't wait to get out of those hideous clothes. This weekend I learned what it was like to be treated like a total piece of shit. I made up my mind right then and there that this wasn't the place for me. I would get up early and make a break for it. Just then, the one-armed guy came into the room and told me I would be going with him the following day to San Diego to work at the main store. I nodded my head, but I knew in my heart that I wasn't going anywhere with that dude. See, I was on formal probation, but I didn't know exactly what that meant. I did know that I wasn't supposed to leave the County of Imperial without permission of the Probation Department. I didn't even have a probation officer or know who to contact. Either way, I wasn't going anywhere with this guy. I decided that I would go to IVC and find someone to let me stay with them until I could get on my feet. This would all work out. In the morning I put on my IVC sweats, packed up my clothes, and bounced out the door, headed for IVC. I asked God to give me strength during the journey. My knee hurt real bad but I blocked out the pain and hit the road. As I walked up the road, I smiled.

Like I said, my knee was really hurting so I decided to hitch a ride. I was on a pretty desolate road but a car would go by about every 5 minutes. As I stuck out my thumb, a truck finally stopped. The guy asked me where I was going and I told him to IVC. When we pulled away he said, "How did you get out here?" I lied and told him that my car broke down. Since I had my IVC sweats on and a sports bag, it was believable enough. We chatted on the way and finally we arrived. I thanked him and jumped out. Well, here I was, the place where this nightmare began. I walked onto campus and sat down on a wall in front of the school. It boggled my mind as I sat there, looking around, and trying to figure out how I could have been going to class, coaching baseball, and working out here just 3 short months ago. Now, I was homeless, penniless, and without any sort of transportation. I couldn't help but think that I was screwed. Heck, even people that were living in their car had it better than me. That was the first time, but certainly not the last time, I compared my situation with the people around me and it made me absolutely sick to my stomach. I just prayed that the Lord would guide my way to a better tomorrow. I had to believe it! I had no choice but to trust and believe God had something in store for me. I looked up and saw Jim driving by, I waved, and he stopped. I ran over to his car and got in. I hadn't seen or talked to him since the night he drove me home after getting the DUI. I told him the whole story about the arrest and my time in jail as we sat in his car outside the Athletic Department. He had a class to teach, so we agreed to meet in his office later. I roamed around campus and talked to people I knew. I ran into the woman's basketball coach Jill and she said, "Wow, that must be some diet you're on, you've lost a lot of weight." I laughed and said, "Yea, stress will do that sometimes." Actually, I really hadn't thought about how I looked. I wandered around until Jim was done with his class. We met up in his office and I knew it was time to start asking the question that I had dreaded the entire morning. I said, "Jim, I'm homeless buddy. I need a place to stay for a while. Can I stay with you until I can get back on my feet?" Jim looked down and said, "I can't. I have all girls in my home. It's just not an option. You really can't ask anyone that has a family because it's just not right. Try to find a single guy that has a spare room." Man, I really hated to put a friend in that position. I felt like shit! I looked at him and said, "I know, you're right, but I'm really in a bind here." He had to go teach another class so we just left it at that. I grabbed my bag and walked out to the baseball field. I sat in the bleachers and started to cry. How did I get here? I was a good guy. I had given players money so they could stay in school and not drop out because of financial troubles. I had offered encouragement to players and students that were struggling. Why me God?! What was I going to do? The thought just overwhelmed me. I was tired, I was scared, I was confused, I was in pain, and most of all I was alone. I went back to the gym and just sat outside. The head custodian, Anthony, walked up and said, "Hey Coach, how you doing bro?" Anthony is a great guy. When he found out that I was going to school to get my degree in Alcohol & Drug Studies, we began talking often about our struggles with beer.

We formed a good friendship and talked honestly with each other. I said, "What's up Anthony?" He sat down and I told him all that had happened and he looked shocked. Here I was, down and out like Boxcar Willie, and I was always his source of inspiration for sobriety. He was so disappointed, and it killed me. But if you decide to pick up a drink, this is where it usually leads eventually, if you are a problem drinker. Which I am. A.A promised jails, institutions, and death if you continued to drink. If you count my trip to the Behavioral Health, I figured I had experienced two of the promises. I refused to complete the trifecta! Anthony had to get back to work, so we hugged he and he took off. Later he returned and said, " Here Coach." And he handed me a twenty dollar bill. I thanked him and hugged him again. I went to the cafeteria, but I wasn't really hungry. I was out of Copenhagen tobacco so I was stressing. I saw two of my players walking across the parking lot so I ran after them, even though my knee hurt like a son of a bitch. I caught up to them and asked them if they would give me a ride to the store. They took me to the store and I bought Copenhagen with the money that Anthony had given me. We returned to the school and I basically just sat around. I saw Anthony up by the gym and I walked up and said, "Anthony, do you think I could stay with you for awhile until I get my affairs in order? He thought about it for a second and finally responded, "Sure Coach, that's cool. We have plenty of room. I get off in about an hour so meet me up at the gym." I felt such relief. I met him up at the gym later and we drove to his house. We went in and he showed me around. Anthony had a beautiful home and it was huge. Maybe now I could relax. We went out to his back yard and he showed me the putting green that he recently put in. Honestly, I was impressed that a custodian had such a beautiful home. I went into the living room and sat in a recliner. Anthony, who is a devote Christian, put a CD on the stereo that was of the book of Jonah. I rested in the recliner and listened to it. Just then, Anthony's wife came home. He told me to just relax and he would go tell her about me being there. After about 15 minutes, he came down stairs and said, "I'm sorry Coach, but you can't stay here." I was crushed! But I understood. I grabbed my bag and we drove back to IVC. Anthony apologized as I got out of his truck and I said, "No problem bro, I understand. Thank you for everything today." And he drove off. I went into the gym and saw Coach Benton, the other woman's basketball coach. I strolled over to him and said, "Hey Mike, does Drew still have his apartment in El Centro? I was referring to Andrew Robinson, the Men's assistant basketball coach. He used to have an apartment with one of our baseball players. Mike said, "No, Drew is living with Coach Aye (the Men's Basketball head coach). I said, "Coach, I need help. I'm homeless and need a place to stay." He looked at me and said, "Are you hungry?" and I said I was. We went to the cafeteria and he bought me a burrito. We went back to the gym and talked for awhile. He told me that, for the night, I could sleep in the coach's office. He showed me around the office, which I knew like the back of my hand. He hugged me and left for the night. I looked around and found some cushions. I laid them out and put a blanket over them. I found another blanket and I was set. I said my prayers and laid down to sleep. I went right out. But I was awoken by someone that opened the coaches door at around 2:00 am. It scared the shit out of me but I remained still. The door closed and I went back to sleep. It's crazy how somewhere you're so familiar with and where you are always welcome, can become a spooky place when you're not supposed to be there. I woke up at 6:00 am not knowing where the hell I was. I shook out the cobwebs and realized that I was in the coaches room at IVC. I placed the cushions back on the sofa and folded up the blankets. Then I picked up my bag and walked across the basketball court to the locker room. I went in and turned on the shower. While the shower was running I shaved in the sink. I went back to the shower and it was still as cold as ice. Since I had no choice, I gritted my teeth, and I showered as quickly as I could. When I was done I shook myself dry and got dressed. I went back to the gym and laid in the bleachers until people started filing in. Anthony came in and handed me a sack lunch that he had prepared for me. I told you he was a special guy. I went to Jim's office. When he came in he said, "I got good news. Coach Deyo knows of a Christian Men's home here in El Centro. Talk to him when he comes in." I said, "Great." Maybe there was hope yet, and I thanked God. When Coach Deyo came in I went to his office. He told me about the home and that if I was interested he would call them. Since I had no choice at that point, I said, "Sure." I went back to Jim's office and sat down at the desk. I was desperate and I said, "Bro, are you sure I can't stay with you? Hell, I'll sleep in the garage if I have to. Please let me stay with you." He said, "Coach, I can't, it's just out of the question." My voice cracked as I said, "I don't want to go to no home. Please." He answered, " What choice do you have? It's either the home or the streets." This was the first time I saw the sorrow on a friend's face because they wanted to help, but just couldn't. And it killed me! I got up and left the office and went back to Coach Deyo's office. Coach Deyo asked, "Do you want me to call the home?" I said,

"Please do." And he dialed the number. I got on the phone with a guy named Pastor Tommie. He asked if I was a Christian and I told him I was. He told me to come on down...Just like Bob Barker on "The Price is Right." Coach Deyo drove me over to the home and I checked into New Creations, a Men's Christian home. I was full of hope and I figured this was just part of God's plan. I had no idea that this wasn't going to be a move towards God's glory, but instead, the beginning of my own personal view of hell on earth, so I smiled.

I walked in and met a guy named Ralph. He gave me some forms to fill out and asked for my identification. I told him that I didn't have any form of I.D because the police had taken my wallet from my home the night I was arrested. I never saw that wallet again and everyone claimed they had no idea where it went. Ralph is a huge man with a big heart. He doesn't say much but you can tell he lives his faith. When I was finished signing all the documents, I turned over my bag with all of my clothes. I was led into a living room where I met a kid named Brian. He was a young guy, about 19 years old, and he knew the Bible real well. I told him a little bit about my experience and he welcomed me. Other guys came in periodically and introduced themselves. From talking to them, I learned most of the rules and procedures in the home. There was no cussing, no smoking or drinking (naturally), no fighting, we go to church every Wednesday and Sunday, we weren't allowed to go outside unless we were going to church, going to work, going to a work call, doing chores, going to Bible study, and we couldn't speak to anyone outside the home if we were outside. That last one seemed ridiculous. I looked around and thought, "How is this not a cult?" After about an hour, Brother Ralph brought me my bag and said it was clean. They had confiscated my Catholic Bible and my tobacco. I didn't appreciate them touching my Bible but, of course, I understood about the tobacco. We went upstairs and entered a room. I was shown to a bunk bed and was told that it was where I would sleep. Ralph told me to rest for a little while and they would call me for dinner. I put my stuff away and laid on the bed. My knee was aching but I just tried to block it out. After an hour or so I decided this wasn't the place for me. Really, I wanted my tobacco. I went downstairs and knocked on the office door. Another counselor named Eddie answered. I told him that I didn't appreciate that they took the liberty of taking my Bible and that I wanted to leave. He tried to persuade me to stay, but my craving for a dip far outmatched anything he could say. He pulled out my bag and I started going through it. I saw my Bible but where was my Copenhagen? Eddie said he dumped it out in the toilet. Oh no you didn't! Since my dip was gone, I started to backtrack. I said to Eddie, "Do you think this is the right place for me?" He said, "If you give it a chance I'm sure you'll love it." I said, "You know what? I think I'll give it a chance." He said, "Well OK, go back to your room and get ready for dinner." I went back upstairs to my room and laid down, feeling like I just dodged a bullet. I didn't have anywhere to go and it was late in the afternoon. A few minutes later, a guy named Raul came in to the room. He introduced himself and we seemed to get along real well. We talked for awhile until they called us for chow time. We went downstairs and into the kitchen. We had to stand in line silently as each brother was given his tray. I was given a tray with two hot dogs, a bag of Sun chips, and some green beans. I walked forward, grabbed a cup, and poured myself some Kool-Aid from a cooler. When everyone was served and sitting in their seat, we prayed. You weren't allowed to speak at the dinner table or you would get written up by one of the interns. They were guys that had been in the home for some time and earned the right to give others discipline. See, every Wednesday night, after Bible study, the counselors would read off your punishments for the past week. Depending on the number of write ups that you had, you would receive different forms of punishment for the following week. They ranged from books, which meant you had to write, word for word, from the book of Proverbs. If you had 5 books that meant you had to write all of the first 5 chapters word for word. If you had 10 books it was the first 10 chapters, and so on. The worst discipline was something they called Moto. It stands for motivation, and consists of not talking to anyone at all, doing dishes after every meal, getting up an hour earlier than anyone else, going to bed an hour later than anyone else, if we were given time off you had to do nothing but read the Bible, and if any undesirable work needed to be done, you would be the guy. It sucked. After dinner I dumped my tray and stacked it by the kitchen. It was becoming apparent that this place was a lot like jail, but you had to work your tail off. I went back to my room and laid down. As much as I loved the Lord and wanted to serve Him, I didn't want to be here, but I had no other place to go. Plus, I had learned that as long as you remained in the home, the probation department wouldn't mess with you. I didn't want to get into any further trouble with the authorities and I certainly didn't want to go back to jail. I was deathly afraid of going back to jail because I saw how easily it is to just get lost in the system. So when I went to sleep that night, I thanked the Lord for giving me a place to sleep. The night before was so uncomfortable because I was afraid that the night custodian would call the police and I would either be arrested or sent to the streets. I was in a place where I was welcome tonight, so I smiled.

The following morning I got dressed and went down to breakfast. We had a bowl of oatmeal and some Kool-Aid. I was called into the office and introduced to my counselor, Leo. He was a nice guy and he told me if I ever needed to talk to feel free to come see him. I told him that my most pressing problem was that I didn't have any form of I.D and I didn't have a Social Security card. That disqualified me from getting any county provided health care and a food stamp card. The food stamp card was taken from all the brothers that entered the home and was supposed to be used to buy food for all of us. I would later find out that this was the most glaring hustle for those in charge. Leo said he would take care of those issues and not to worry. A week later, Leo got in some type of hot water with the elders of the church and he left the home. Now what? You know, this type of thing seemed to happen to me a lot. In fact, the priest that baptized me when I was 30 years old in the Catholic church, left the church a month later to get married. Brother Ralph became my counselor but he had no idea how I could get an I.D without having the money to pay for it at the Department of Motor Vehicles. I was back to square one. So here was the breakdown of New Creations. It was run by a church called Christ Community Church and it's head pastor was Pastor Walter, a former heroin addict. He had other pastors on staff like Pastor Tommie, a former cocaine addict and dealer. Pastor Frank, a former heroin addict. Pastor Chris, a clean cut kid with no shady past that I was aware of and Pastor Dennis, a real nice guy and I never learned his past. The Men's home, which was located across the street from the church, was a refurbished motel. When it was a motel, Pastor Tommie used to sell drugs there, and actually was arrested there for dealing. Tommie was a real piece of work. He never quite outgrew his hustling attitude. He was just pimpin for the Lord now. He was once caught red handed using the brother's food stamp cards to buy food for his own use at home and he lied right to Pastor Walt's face when he was confronted about it. I've been around long enough to recognize a bullshitter, and I never trusted that dude. Pastor Frank was a quiet spoken Man of God in my eyes from Calexico. He always walked the walk and worked tirelessly for the Youth Ministry. Like I said, I never really got to know Pastors Chris and Dennis. A typical day at New Creations went as follows. We would wake up at 6:00 am and go to the "chapel", which was a little room located in the backyard. We would be required to pray for 30 minutes and then someone would get up and do a devotion that lasted 15 minutes. We then walked to the kitchen to eat breakfast that usually consisted of oatmeal, pancakes, or cereal. When we were done, 3 people would be chosen to do the dishes. But before anyone could do anything we were required to clean our rooms, top to bottom. After inspection of the rooms by the interns we had to gather again in the chapel. At that point, one of the interns would assign chores to everyone. The chores consisted of things like vacuuming, doing the dishes (if you were one of the 3 chosen after breakfast), cleaning the windows inside and out, picking up trash and raking the grounds around the home, cleaning the chapel, cleaning all the downstairs toilets, and mopping the dining hall. The chores would usually last about an hour and then we would return to the chapel for Bible study. Sometimes the home would bring in a speaker and other times one of the counselors would do it. Bible study lasted an hour, then we returned to our rooms to put away our Bibles. After that, like always, we went to the chapel to be assigned our job for the day. The main job in the home was to work at the New Creations car wash. Also we had a 3 man lawn crew, they were the same 3 people until they were removed from the crew. 3 people worked at another church in Brawley. We worked at our job until 5:00 pm and returned to the home. Oh, by the way, when we went to our job we were given the same damn bologna sandwich everyday. When we got back to the house, it was time for dinner. We would eat in silence and then take a shower. After showers were done we would meet in the chapel for Bible study. After Bible study we would pray for 30 minutes and then you could do one of three things. You could sleep, read the Bible, or pray. And that was a typical day at New Creations. I really enjoyed the Bible study and praying, but everything else about the home sucked. I mean this wasn't like a church in any way. How could it be? We had drug abusers, alcoholics (hand sanitizer was prohibited because some drunks would drink it), drug dealers, con men, murderers, perpetrators of violent crimes, thieves, rapists, etc. And most of them were court ordered to be there, so they were pissed that they had to be there. My experience was different from most of the other brothers because I didn't have to be there. I just didn't have anywhere else to go. It started to depress me deeply because I didn't see any way out. I wasn't allowed to look for a job, so that I could pull myself up, after putting myself in that position. I dreaded the thought of staying here forever but that looked like a real possibility. The fact of the matter was that I needed a place to stay, to find a job, work until I could save enough to find my own place, and only then would I be in a position to leave the Valley and return to San Diego when my probation was up. I didn't have a place to stay and I wasn't allowed to call anyone or even talk to anyone outside the home. I was just plain stuck. I didn't want to be like brother Ralph, a lifer that had never held a job in his entire life (his words, not mine). All of the house staff had been to prison except brother Ralph, who had been to jail and got booked so bad that he vowed never to return. So they weren't counselors, they were really preaching guards. Period! The more I thought about the predicament that I was in, the more depressed I became. It really came to a head one day at the car wash when I slipped off of a step ladder and really messed up my knee. I could barely stand on it. That night I couldn't even sleep because of the pain. At 5:00 am I heard the train whistle from outside and I knew it was close to wake up time. I would learn to hate that whistle because it signaled that another brutal day was about to begin. On this day, since I hadn't slept all night, I was particularly stressed. I brushed my teeth and went down to breakfast. After breakfast I was sitting on the couch in the living room. Suddenly, I felt a sharp pain in my chest. I doubled over and Raul asked if I was alright. I told him, "No bro, I think I'm having a heart attack." Since I had told him that I was concerned because I didn't have my high blood pressure medication since I left jail, he jumped up and ran to tell the staff that I was having a heart attack. Some of the brothers carried me to the van and they rushed me to the hospital. A nurse shoved some nitroglycerine down my throat and they examined me. My blood pressure was 203/155. They hooked me up to an I.V and gave me Ativan. After about 30 minutes I was feeling better. They came in to get my information, and I was utterly embarrassed. They asked questions like, What is your address? I answered, "I don't know." They continued, "What is your phone number?' I said, "I don't know." On and on it went, insurance? No. Marital status? Separated. Family to notify? None. Employer? None. The nurse finally just gave up. I was a nobody! I didn't have any I.D, I didn't have family, I didn't have a place of residence, and I didn't have a phone number. I basically didn't exist! If I didn't know it prior to that moment, I was perfectly aware now, that I had hit rock bottom. Raul finally came in the room and gave the nurse my address and phone number. So like they do with every person that doesn't have insurance, they discharged me immediately. I was given a prescription for Ativan and another for Tylenol with Codeine for my knee. Raul said there was no reason to fill them because they wouldn't allow me to take them anyway. I agreed because I had no money or insurance. We drove back to the home in silence. I went to my room and laid down. Soon after that, brother Ralph came in and said he once had the same thing happen to him. He said I could have the day off and to get some rest. Since I hadn't hardly slept in 4 days, I fell right to sleep. Maybe this would make them aware of my medical condition and they would help me obtain medical insurance. I'm not absolutely sure, because I was in dreamland, but I think I smiled.

At New Creations it is truly believed that anything and everything can be prayed away. In regards to my knee, it wasn't working. But I got up every morning and did what I was told to do. I had been there for two weeks and wasn't living, but only existing. One morning while I was cleaning my room I got called down to the office. I knocked on the door and Eddie opened it. There was Sandra standing there. I walked over and hugged her. It seems Mitz had sent her there to have me sign our 2009 tax return. I had already decided that I had to forgive her to move on with my life. I signed the return and asked Sandra to give the boys a hug for me. She said she would, and she left. You should have seen the staff guys stare at her when she left. You would think they never saw a woman before. Eddie said, "Wow Coach, you sure know how to pick them." I glared at him and said, "That's my friend's wife." And I walked out. By the way, I never saw any of the money that we had coming from our taxes. I was essentially on the street and Mitz didn't even consider floating me a few bucks. She is a cold piece of work! Up until that point, I had a lower bunk bed without anyone sleeping above me. But today that would change. A homeless guy came into the home. I mean this guy was as dirty and smelly as a human being could be. He reeked of alcohol and he had that crazy look in his eyes like some drunks do. Sure enough, he was assigned to the bunk above me. Even after he showered he still looked dirty. I tried not to judge him but it was hard because he was hateful, bitter, and rude. His name was Robert and he was a frequent visitor to places like this. He had that rusty look of someone who had spent many days in the sun and many nights face down in the gutter. The first night was the worst. His feet would hang over the end of the bed and his green toenails would be right above my face. He also would fart and it was like he was shitting on my head. It was so gross and it disgusted me to no end. The following night I came out of the shower and Robert was sitting in the middle of the floor, wearing my glasses, and clipping his green, two inch toenails. I walked up and snatched my glasses off his dirty ass head and said, "Don't ever touch anything of mine without asking, you understand?" He just looked up and said, "Whatever." Then he went back to flinging those damn boomerangs all over the room. Two days later, they kicked him out of the home. I had begun worrying about the fact that I didn't have any money to buy simple things like soap, toothpaste, razors, and shaving cream. I told brother Ralph and he said, "You do have money." I said, "From where?" and he said, "From Coach Deyo and Coach Benton." I said, "How much?" He answered, "I don't know, they gave it to Pastor Tommie at church Sunday." I said, "Was he ever going to tell me?" He said, "I don't know." So the next day I asked Tommie, "Hey did Coach Deyo and Coach Benton give you money for me?" He said, "Oh yeah, I forgot to tell you, I'll give it to brother Ralph." I said, "Thanks." I knew that son of a bitch was no good. I immediately put my name on the list to go on the next store run. When that night came, we all loaded into the van and went to Wal-Mart. Eddie had all of our money in individual envelopes. When I got up to the counter I asked him for my money. He said, "I got it." I said, "You're going to pay for it?" He said, "Yes." After they rang up my toothbrush, razors, deodorant, toothpaste, and hard candy, Eddie pulled out an envelope with my name on it, and took the money out. He wasn't going to pay for it out of his money, he was paying for it out of my money. I stood there, a grown ass man, and I had to have a reformed attempted murderer pay for my shit with my money. Along with not being able to talk to anyone that I knew on the street, I now had to have someone handle my money for me? It's fucking dehumanizing! Not to mention childish. I already had my share of embarrassing moments because of this no talking bullshit. One day at the car wash a girl from my classes at IVC came to get her car washed. Her name was Desiree and she usually would sit in front of me in most of our classes. Desiree sat down and was waiting for her car and she looked over at me. Since there were interns around, and I didn't want to get written up, I went and hid in the port-a-john until she left. Another time was at church on a Wednesday night. Another girl from my class was sitting behind me. She said, "Hi Coach." And I looked over my left shoulder and waived. That time I did get written up by this asshole intern named Vince. Seems we're not supposed to look around at church...eyes straight ahead. I had to write 5 books for that one. But the worst time was at this function at IVC that I definitely didn't want to go to. That day sucked! We were there to be slaves to anyone that needed help setting up or tearing down their booths. The fact that I knew so many people there, it was going to be difficult not to talk to anyone. I didn't want them to see me like this.

Sure enough, when we got out of the van and walked over to the gym, I started seeing everyone I knew. Pedro, the baseball coach at Brawley, walked up and said, "What's up coach?" I said, "Hey Pete, I'm in this program and can't talk to anyone. Take care buddy." He said, "Alright, take care of yourself." Right then Raul (who was now an intern) came up to me and said, "Eddie, if you want to talk to someone just come get me and we'll meet them in the bathroom." Oh, that was another thing, you couldn't go the bathroom without an intern. They called it your accountability. I saw Anthony go in the gym, and I went and got Raul, and he agreed to come with me. We went in the gym and Anthony lit up when he saw me. He came over and I gave him a big hug. I said, "Listen bro, I need to thank you for all you did for me. I really appreciate it." He said, "I know you would do the same for me bro." We chatted for a minute and then Raul said we had to go. Anthony looked at Raul and said, "Thank you for taking care of my brother, man." Raul said, "No problem." And we left and went back to our band of misfits. I never wanted to venture out of the home again. But at least seeing a couple of familiar faces made me smile a little bit. I was becoming a real pain to be around. I was constantly depressed because I saw no hope in my life whatsoever. And I really tried to find a ray of hope while in this position. But as I wrote about it and thought about it, I always ended up with the same outcome...I was screwed. I once heard that depression is the emotional result of hopelessness. Joy is the emotional result of hope. Peace is the emotional result of faith. Well, I had no hope, so I was depressed and I had absolutely no joy. All I could see wherever I looked was more of the same and I hated it! I studied the word of God intently and I still had faith in Him. But I had no faith in myself. In my eyes, I only had two choices, either stay here or leave and become a bum on the streets. I wasn't going to give up, my sons needed me. So I continued to just exist. The brief moments of peace that I experienced came from my faith in Jesus Christ. But no question, I was struggling with the forces of evil on a daily basis. Everyone that I met attempted to cheer me up and encourage me, but after they heard my story, they would just walk away mumbling, "That guy's fucked." Besides being stuck in this house of horrors, I still had to resolve my DUI case in court. Brother Ralph would take me to court and the prosecutor was pushing for jail time for a third offense. I was deathly afraid to return to jail. All it takes in jail is one asshole to push the right buttons and I could get into a fight that would earn me additional time. I didn't want to chance it. Hell, I wanted this thing to be over with. It's just too damn easy to get lost in the system down there in Mexican Mayberry. I had met enough people down there that started off with one simple charge, and with probation violations, they had become frequent fliers at the county jail. A second home if you will. I was going to do anything that I could to avoid going any lower than I already was.

In the home, we were given a list of 20 memory scriptures. Every Wednesday, we would be tested on them. Your first week you had to write down the first scripture perfectly. The address and the scripture, word for word. The second week, you would write the first and the second scripture, and so on. The longer you stayed there, the more difficult it became. If you messed up on one, you were placed on academic discipline. You would then be required to write the scripture(s) that you missed 100 times and have to turn it in. We also had homework. The sheets were so poorly written that you had no idea what they wanted for an answer. Hell, they were written by cons and drug addicts, what the fuck did they know about academia? I bet you could count on one hand how many of them that had graduated high school. I became friends with a guy named Cliff. I knew his brother Robert, who played in the NFL, because he spent a lot of time around IVC sporting events. Cliff was an ex-police officer that suffered from PTSD after a violent shooting that he was involved in. He had went back to school to get his Master's and he was most recently a high school teacher. We would look at the homework sheets, then turn to each other with a look of, What the fuck? We would do this while sitting in "Study Hall." Study Hall? What the hell do these mental midgets know about Study Hall? It was a joke! But like everything else, no matter how stupid it was, we had to do it. I would just write long, drawn out answers that had nothing to do with the question, and Tommie would write things on my papers like, "Profound" or "Very insightful" and stuff like that. I once wrote, "Like the wings of the African sparrow take root in the confinement of the latter-day saints roaming at mach speed throughout the wilderness on high. The Apostle Paul attained eclectic, visionary predominance over monolithic obedience that he had previously overlooked." Pastor Tommie wrote, "Definitely divinely inspired" on my paper, but of course he misspelled both definitely and inspired. I figured the African part would hook him since he was a black dude. I became friends with other good guys in my 7 months in the home. Guys like Ryan. Ryan had previously served in the Army and was trained in Nuclear Medicine. He was a radiation tech at the local hospital. He was one smart dude and he didn't take any shit from anyone including staff.

They would give him as many books to write as they wanted and he would knock them out without batting an eye. He would just say, "They can't break me, it's just not going to happen." Ryan was a white guy and he didn't like Pastor Tommie and Pastor Tommie didn't like him. It was obvious that Ryan knew Tommie was a fake, a hustler, and a con man and Tommie was resentful because he knew that Ryan had him pegged from the start. And Ryan wasn't afraid to show it. I knew it too, but since I didn't have anywhere to go, I kept my mouth shut. Ryan had a circulation problem in his legs which would cause him severe pain and swelling from the knee down. His legs would get so swelled and purple that one time at the car wash a woman threatened to report the home to the authorities for abuse, after seeing his legs. But Ryan never showed any reaction at all. He just kept scrubbing the bugs off the fenders. The car wash was known to provide excellent service for a mere $8.00. That included a hand wash that included complete bug removal (which was extensive in the desert), vacuum and detail inside, windows cleaned inside and out, rims polished, and tires coated with Armor-all. You can do that when you don't have to pay the employees a dime. Ryan had been there for 11 and a half months on a one year sentence. Tommie came down hard on him one day for disagreeing with him. Ryan put him in check and Tommie kicked him out. Can you believe that shit? Ryan simply told him that he thought he was wrong and he bounced him. You have to be a cold motherfucker to mess with someone's life like that. But in typical Ryan fashion, he simply packed his stuff and had his wife come pick him up. Oh, no she didn't pick him up at the home because Tommie wouldn't allow him to use the phone. Ryan had to hump all his stuff down to the store and use a pay phone. But that wouldn't be the last time we would see Ryan. On Saturday, which is the day we all worked at the car wash (all day), Ryan pulled into the car wash to have his car washed. He got out of the car smoking a cigarette and said, "Now make it shine fellas." He was standing in the waiting area and said, "Remember guys, as you can see, you'll never make it on the outside. You have no chance without the guidance of the mighty Pastor Tommie, who is being investigated for fraud of your food stamp cards." I couldn't stop laughing. I didn't care if I got written up, this shit was funny. When his car was finished he drove next door to Burger's and Beer, a local sports pub. He had a cigarette and a draft beer while he stood on the patio of the club. He would pop off every now and then saying, "Hey Ed, Oklahoma is playing Nebraska, come over and I'll buy you a cold one. Hey, I know you're making good money over there, but live a little." I was laughing my ass off. That dude was one of a kind. I've recently gotten back in touch with him on Facebook and he told me that he had to serve a whole year in another Men's home because of Tommie's bullshit.

Speaking of Burger's and Beer, it was less than 50 yards from the car wash. I would often see friends going in and out of there. I would kind of hide because I didn't want them to see me. I looked like shit because I had begun to wear the same pair of shorts everyday and they were grungy. My glasses had a few chips in them from sitting on them or dropping them. I looked like a skeleton and probably smelled because when I ran out of deodorant or toothpaste, I just went without, I had no choice, because mooching off the other brothers gets embarrassing. This asshole in the home named Angel began calling me Waldo (as in Where's Waldo) because of my chipped glasses and tore up haircut. In truth, I really kind of looked like the motherfucker. So I had begun hiding if I saw anyone I knew. But the worst Saturday at the car wash was the first one. A lot of the Pop Warner football teams gathered there after games. The first time I saw a youngster that played for Calexico (Mark and Robert's league) I almost lost it. I thought, "How the hell did I get here? It was only 4 months ago and that was me. Coaching their teams and going out to lunch afterwords." It stung my heart like crazy. I couldn't help but to shed a tear and feel the sense of loss.

The car wash had a number of different stations. You had the wash bay, the vacuum, the dry bay, windows, door jams and dashes, and wheels and tires. Dry bay was the best because you just had to  dry off the car with a shammy. Everything else sucked! It would often times be 109 or 110 degrees and to do anything inside the car like vacuum, the windows, or dashes was miserable. But by far, the worst was the wash bay. You basically had to do the bulk of the wash. You had to wet the cars down, scrub all the bugs off of the entire car with a brush and a bucket of soap, scrub the roof of the car which often meant climbing on a ladder, washing the car with a scrub rag, and rinsing the car. It fuckin sucked! Everyone knew I had a bad knee so I spent most days in dry bay, but that involved climbing a ladder, so I was always in pain. On Saturdays, the cars would be lined up a hundred yards deep, and we had to do them quickly, but perfectly. If you missed a spot you would get written up for, now get this, not working unto the Lord. One time a guy I knew from USG came in named Ruben. When I worked there we were pretty tight. He brought his piece of shit truck in and I was on dashes. After he was done he drove away. He returned a short time later and complained that his dash was still dirty. The interns look over and I'm on dashes. This asshole named Johnny came over and told me that he had a complaint. I look at the truck and then at Ruben. Since I couldn't say what I wanted to say, which was, "What the fuck are you doing bro? This truck is a piece of shit! Don't you know I'm going to get written up for this?" I just glared at him. He gave me the Calexico salute, which was to throw his hands up and shrug, like saying, What? If I saw him today, since I'm a Christian and don't whoop no ass anymore, I would rebuke his ass in the name of the Lord. There is a difference, figure it out! After I was in the home for a couple of months some of the guys got resentful because I didn't have to work in the wash bay because of my knee. Well, when they eventually became interns they purposely assigned me to the wash bay on the worst day, Saturday. On Saturdays we would arrive at 7:00 am and worked the entire day until 5:00 pm, non-stop. It was the worst. This one guy in the home was named Raymond. This dude was the phoniest guy I ever met. He was the type that would be your friend one minute and talk shit and stab you in the back the next. He was all tatted up and thought he was an O.G. in the Mexican Mafia. What Raymond didn't realize was that he was an old man, he wasn't cool, and he certainly wasn't a tough guy. What he was, was an agitator that liked to start trouble and then step away. According to his tats he had been in prison over half of his life. He was a drug addict and probably had never been in a fight. I learned from a few guys that Raymond was a PC. That meant he would go Protective Custody when he was locked up. PC is the worst thing you could do in jail. You would be identified in bright red jumpsuits and you are hated by everyone. Most child abusers (chomos), rats, etc. were in PC. So when old man Ray became an intern, he would put me in wash bay every Saturday. Like Angel, I began to actually hate Ray. If I saw them today, I believe a rebuking would be in order. But back then, since there was no fighting allowed in the home, I just smiled.

The cast of characters that came in and out of New Creations were interesting, to say the least. There were some good guys like Adam, Justin, Pepe, Dustin, Bruce, and Rayburn. Bruce and I got along real well because he was a Crip from San Diego. We knew a lot of the same people and we shared one major experience in the home, and that was racism. Whether they realize or not, the Imperial Valley is full of racist assholes, and if you're not Mexican you are singled out. So since Bruce was African American and I was white, and we were not from Mexican Mayberry, we were looked down upon. Never mind that most of those punks wouldn't last a day in our neighborhood. They always had us outnumbered so we just went with it. One white guy that they didn't mess with was Rayburn. He was a mammoth farm boy and he was from the Valley. He had some problems with drugs but he was also very strong (He actually played football at San Diego State at one time). Dude was tough as hell. At the car wash, he would kill horseflies and eat them. Sometimes he would catch lizards out in the backyard and he would immediately bite it's head off. He was a trip. But overall, I got along with most of the people that came through the home. All, except one. His name was Jose and he was a convicted child molester. I just couldn't get past that fact. Jose had been in the home for a long time, but now he was living at his sister's house. When the law came out that child molesters couldn't reside within a certain distance from schools, Jose was forced to leave the home since there was a school located across the street from the home. But he would often show up at the car wash and at the home. One time he was left at the home with one other guy and he invited two kids in. That could have been a disaster for those in charge but luckily nothing happened since someone came home and rebuked his ass. I believe wholeheartedly in the Lord's forgiveness and redeeming power, but this dude wasn't reformed and had no business being around children. I just couldn't get past what this guy had done, and would do again, if given the chance. I would be remiss if I didn't mention the mature gentlemen in the home. One was a guy named Derek. Derek was a farmer, he was tough, and he had a heart of gold. I saw him often sit and care for brothers that came into the home that were kicking heroin or meth. Those guys would really be suffering and he would take care of them completely. He really lived his faith. I actually served on the civil grand jury with his brother and coached his nephew at IVC. He would always tell me that things would work out and that I'd be alright, and I appreciated it, but I also knew the reality of the situation and as I've mentioned, I was screwed and destined to be like the Seinfeld character that was George's coach and had ended up on the street as a homeless man. Remember? He used to refer to George as Cantstandya instead of Costanza. Well that was where I was going and I hated it! The other elder statesman was a guy named Ben Gay. Yep, that was his given name. Ben was the cook and could be a salty son of a bitch, but he also had a good heart. I really respected the character of those two men.

I continued to go to court for my DUI case and after the fourth trip the prosecutor finally offered to give me 6 months in the home, instead of the mandatory 4 months in jail. I jumped on it! I had already served 5 months there, so that meant after one more month, the case would be resolved. I felt good about it because it made my time in that hell hole worthwhile. I would still have fines and 10 days of community service, but I didn't have jail hanging over my head anymore.

I read inspirational books whenever I had a chance and worshiped the Lord with all of my heart. I was crumbling from the inside out, literally. I searched so hard to find that door of hope in my valley of trouble, but it just wasn't there. Facts were facts. When Cliff was getting ready to leave the home we were talking in the chapel one afternoon. I said, "Cliff, when you go home, will you do me a favor?" He said, "Sure." I said, "Bro, don't judge me, but will you bring me a gun." I assumed that since he was an ex-police officer that he had firearms. He said, "Eddie, you can't do that, you have your sons to think of bro." I replied, " I'll never see them again. I have nothing to give them and I just don't ever see it happening. I'm through bro and I can't stand this stuff anymore. Just help me out." He said, "I don't know how it's going to work out for you, but you're too good of a man for it not to. Just hang on and don't lose hope." What he didn't realize was that I lost all hope a long time ago. My thoughts were mainly about how I would end my life and hoped that God would have mercy on me for taking the coward's way out. The sorrow I felt just hurt so deep. When I would read the Bible and came to a scripture that dealt with marriage or relationships, I would just skip over them because I knew that I would probably never be with a woman ever again. What woman would ever want to be with a total loser like me? In my mind, this wasn't a self pity party, it was just fact. I had pretty much lost all sex drive and was suffering from such deep depression that having any sort of relations with a woman was completely out of the question. We had Bill and Pam Farrel, who wrote "Men are like waffles, Women are like spaghetti" come to our church to speak and it was entertaining, but as far as applying it to my life, it wasn't in the cards for me. So Cliff and I just left it there and never spoke of it again.

I had been in the home for 5 months and was basically a shell of my former self. It was getting close to the National Day of Prayer and we went out daily to put up signs announcing the event that was to be held at Southwest High School in El Centro. We loaded the van on the day of the event and went to the school. It was a huge auditorium and there were a lot of people in attendance. I was stressing because we were to perform there. That's a big thing at New Creations. Not only were you required to work your ass off, but we also had to participate in choir. It was brutal. We would have choir practice all the time and whenever there was an event in town we were required to perform like dancing monkeys. I hated that shit! Why? Because I was the fuckin lead singer! My stupid ass was belting it out one day at practice, just messing around, and the choir director tapped me for the lead singers position. I didn't want to do it and I tried to beg off, but like anything else in the home, what you think, feel, or want to do doesn't matter in the slightest. Fact was, we were fuckin slaves to these zealots and you could accept it or get on down the road. If there was an event around town, two things were certain. We would be working our asses off and we would be performing like the Jailbird Tabernacle Choir. So at the National Day of Prayer we got together in small groups and prayed. I was in a group with Angel and Adam. We were petitioning to the Lord and Angel was really getting down. He was saying (actually yelling) shit like, "Father, please heal the heterosexuals!" Of course he meant the homosexuals, but who the fuck was listening anyway? But when he said it, I looked at Adam and he was starting to laugh. We tried our best to hold it, but it was impossible, we both hit our knees and slammed our heads into our theater seats and rolled our asses off. I couldn't stop laughing because Angel was such a phony motherfucker and he was also dumb as hell. Naturally, we couldn't let anyone see us laughing, so we just remained squatted in our seats laughing hysterically. Well, I paid the price for that one. Not by any discipline from an intern or pastor, but by karma. See, we weren't exposed to any type of outside media or television at all, written or otherwise. But since we were involved in the National Day of Prayer event, someone brought the front page of the Imperial Valley Press into the home. Right there on the front page, bigger than life, was a picture of me singing like some Smokey Robinson reject. I was humiliated and just hoped no one recognized me. This happened before Ryan was kicked out of the home. Ryan wasn't going to miss this opportunity to rag me. He grabbed the paper and pretended to read the caption. He announced, "IVC baseball coach, Eddie Richey, sings to the masses gathered at Southwest High for the National Day of Prayer." I couldn't help but to laugh. He wasn't done though. He went on, "Mr. Richey is available to perform for free at any weddings, funerals, or kiddie parties. If interested, please contact his spiritual adviser, Brother Ralph, at New Creations Christian's Men's Home where Coach Richey is currently serving a 6 month sentence for threatening to kill his wife and multiple DUI convictions." Now I was rolling. I told you, Ryan was hilarious. So that was the deal with the choir, every Wednesday we had to go to an old folks home and sing to the poor old people there, which probably had them begging for the end to come quickly. We sucked!

A guy came running into the home one afternoon and he was shouting, "Everybody get down here right now. Pastor Frank has an emergency at the church. We need to hurry, let's go!" We all lined up on the sidewalk like little soldiers and marched down to the church at the end of the block. There, in the parking lot of the church, was the biggest pile of trash that I have ever seen, outside of a landfill. The pile was at least 8 feet high and 30 yards in diameter. Pastor Frank came out of the church and gave us our orders. We were to pick up everything, clean it off and separate it into like piles to be moved into the church. What? It was 115 degrees outside and we were supposed to pick up this pile of trash? Yep. It seems that a local Big Lots store was closing it's doors, and all of it's merchandise was gathered up in a big rig and donated to Christ Community Church. I couldn't believe what I was hearing. There was  smashed Twinkies, opened packages of Little Debbie snack cakes, cracked bottles of hand soap, etc. It was a trash pile and we had to pick it up one item at a time, and clean it off with a towel and told to organize it. It was brutal. So for the next week, any free time we may have had, was spent at the trash pile. It was gross. The church leaders would come pick up anything that looked usable and take it as a charitable offering to people that were needy. Excuse me assholes, but the real needy folks are right here under your nose! After a hard day at work, in 115 degree heat, you might get "blessed" with a spoiled Little Debbie Oatmeal Cream. Get the fuck out of here! It was the same at the car wash, they had to have this long drawn out tribunal if someone would come along and offer to buy us a soda. But that's the way it was at the home. They just held brothers down to let them know that they were the shit of society, but they promoted themselves to outsiders as a place of restoration for troubled men. One time we did an event for some group's charity dinner. The guys had worked at the dinner for 14 hours and the folks were so grateful that they donated the left over food to the home. Like always, Tommie would oversee the so called donation and he would take inventory of all the food. Well it seems that there was a missing slice, about a three inch by three inch piece, of tri-tip steak. These guys had worked 14 hours and they had shared this piece of steak between the four of them. You would have thought they just robbed a bank. Tommie made it a big deal and he rebuked all four of them severely. They were put on Moto and given 10 books each. For a bite of steak? We dubbed them the "Tri-Tip Cartel" and there was nothing they could say because they were on Moto. Guess it was funny, and sad at the same time.

On Easter Sunday of 2010, we attended morning service as usual. I was really tired and depressed, but I participated in the service and prayed, like I always did, that my heavenly Father would protect my sons Mark and Robert and reunite us as soon as possible. After the service we lined up outside the church, like we always did, and walked back to the home. When I got to my room I pulled off my pitiful black slacks and my stained white shirt and laid in my cot. As I sat there, I once again reviewed my predicament, and came to the same conclusion that I always did. I was fucked! I closed my eyes and said, "Father, I have all the faith in you, your power, and your mercy. Lord, I've obviously offended you to the point that you have turned your eyes from me and left me to suffer. Jesus, I can't go on any longer. I'm sorry for not fulfilling your plan for me and you know it grieves my heart. Lord, I have nothing left, so please end my pitiful existence, and take me from this miserable place." Right then, the room shook so violently that I had to hold on to the bed posts to keep from toppling off. The dresser in the room fell over and the mirror on top of it shattered on the floor. The floor beneath me cracked loud and split into a hole in the middle of the room. One of the other bunks bounced and smashed on it's side. I was so scared and I held my breath. I tried to yell, but instead I just mouthed the words Jesus. And finally it stopped. I laid there wondering if I was in heaven or not. I closed my eyes and said, "Jesus, please give me discernment as to what I'm experiencing. If I've offended you, Father, that was not my intention. Please help me." I was so frightened and was literally numb. It seemed like my body was still shaking, but as I looked down to my arms, I was perfectly still. After about 5 minutes I willed myself out of the bed and looked out the window. Some of the brothers were laughing out in the backyard and others were scurrying around. It was surreal! El Centro had just suffered an 8.5 earthquake and I was definitely a believer in the power and might of Jesus Christ. The Pastor, Walt, came over to the home and made sure everyone was all right. The brothers in the back yard talked about how cool it was to see the cars on the streets bounce like a low-rider and the trees to shake so bad that the branches were just falling off. In the following days it was discovered that the church had suffered such considerable damage that it was condemned. That Easter Sunday was the final service ever held at that church. It would have to be demolished. Guess who would do the grunt work of that operation? You got it, us. The following week's services were held in the park. After that, the church negotiated a two year contract with Southwest High School to hold it's Sunday service at the school. I may be wrong, but I thought that there was a separation between church and state, and this would be in violation. But like anything else in the Valley, if you had the money and the influence, you could do whatever the hillbillies allowed you to do...fuck the law! Now our Sundays would be spent waking up at 5:00 am and going to unload all of the church equipment off of a tractor trailer and set up at the high school, then we would return home to eat breakfast, then get ready for church. It sucked. Then after church, we would take off our ties, and load the truck up with the equipment and only then could we return to the home. Which was way after all other parishioners were long gone. The whole thing had gotten so ridiculous that I couldn't help but to smile.

After the earthquake, all attention was placed on the tearing down of the church. After breakfast each day, we would march over to the church and begin work. There were signs that said, "Keep Out. Danger, Do Not Enter." I guess those were for any person besides us. We were told to go in and sweep for the first two hours. This scared the shit out of me because, not only was the building condemned, but chunks of the roof would often slam to the floor and we didn't have as much as a hard hat. I didn't have any medical insurance, so if I took one to the dome I would be lucky to get a towel for my wound. We were required to go up in the bell tower and remove grating from the frames. For this we had the most unsteady ladders that you ever saw. If I ever hit my knees in the morning and was driven by the Holy Spirit to carry on and have faith, it was crushed when I got to the church site in the morning when we were sent in to this condemned area and shown, without a doubt, that we were expendable, worthless, no account pieces of shit. We were in charge (led by Rayburn) of unbolting the pews and carrying them out, stripping all molding, removing all fixtures, etc. We basically stripped the entire structure. So I figured this was how I would die, crushed in a temple of God, and since I was suicidal anyways I couldn't help but to smile.

Since I had no clothes besides one pair of shorts that I wore every day and three t-shirts, brother Ralph agreed to take me to retrieve the rest of my belongings in Calexico at the apartment complex in which Mitz and I lived. Ralph really appreciated the fact that I didn't nag him about going there even though he was aware that I needed clothes. I had been there for 6 months and now, finally, we were going to pick up all that I owned. Ralph and I drove towards Calexico on Highway 111 when suddenly a woman pulled out in front of us. Ralph swerved to avoid her but nailed her in the left rear. This sent us off the road and spinning in the sand. The woman was knocked through two fences and came to a stop. I wasn't scared at all. To tell the truth, I spent most of my time trying to figure out a way that could end my life that would be relatively painless, but honorable. I didn't ever want my sons to think that I gave up and took my life. But if I was killed in a crash, that wasn't our fault, well OK. I know it's pitiful, but that's where I was. We went to check on the woman and she was OK. After talking to the Officer and giving him the rundown, he determined that it was the woman's fault. Ralph was really shook up, but I assured him that he did nothing wrong. It's interesting to see how a man of faith reacts in a sheltered environment like the home, and then how he reacts when his ass is on fire in an unfamiliar world like real life. We eventually called Pastor Frank and he picked us up. He took me to the complex and I loaded all of my stuff. We returned to the home and I unloaded my things and stored them in Ralph's room. The interesting thing was that the powers that be wouldn't let me go through my clothes and get decent things to wear. I continued to wear the same green Dickie's shorts and rotated my three t-shirts. You can tell that that piece of shit Tommie had something to do with that decision. But Ralph kept my personal affects for over 9 months in his tiny room for me and never said a thing. Like I said, Ralph lives his faith. And I know that if he was aware that the three trunks in his closet were worth $15,000 in vintage baseball memorabilia, it wouldn't have changed a thing.

What ultimately turned out to be my final month at the New Creations home, was eye-opening and eventful to, say the least. It started with a murder/suicide in El Centro. It seems a young female elementary school teacher was divorcing her husband. She and her soon to be ex-husband were meeting behind a store to exchange their 8-year old son for the child to spend time with with father. The husband exited his truck and walked over to the teacher's car. Their 8-year old son was in the backseat of her car. The man shot the young lady in the chest and continued to empty the pistol into her, naturally leaving her dead. He returned to his vehicle, reloaded, and put one in his head. All while this innocent 8-year old boy watched in horror. Tragic! This was another rare occasion that we were shown the news. The man was a family friend of Ben's and the school teacher was a member of Christ Community Church. In the following days we were informed that we would work at the memorial for both of the dead people. When we got there it was so sad. I was posted at the front door handing out programs for the memorial. People were so sad as they entered, of course. It dawned on me that this was why I was here. This shit really happened. Even though I had absolutely no intentions of harming Mitz, the cops didn't know that. From that point on, in regards to my arrest, I accepted my crime and never felt victimized again. When I saw their 8-year old son, I went to the restroom, and cried my eyes out. I thanked God for preventing me from causing this much hurt to so many innocent victims. I returned to the front door and continued to hand out the programs. One of my players from IVC, Matt, came walking up. We hugged and he told me that the teacher was one of his former instructors. I said, "Hey, my life is pretty much over, but know that I tried." He looked at me and said, "Coach, you look great, do you big dog." He probably will never know, until now, how much that lifted my spirits. Hell, it wasn't over for me! I wasn't out. I was just down. I wasn't sitting in a jail or prison cell. Fuck this, I'm Eddie Richey dammit! I don't bow down to no one, and I certainly don't quit. Yep! Hey Satan, take your flaming darts and shove them up your ass! I looked at that poor little boy's grieving face and I mentally promised him that I would never give up, and no way in hell would I be the cause of that pain to anyone...especially my precious sons. Through my tears, I smiled.

Unfortunately, things were the same in the home. It was set up to crush your spirit. Personally, there is no greater crime than to beat someone's spirit and soul down. No one has that right! Still, it happened. There was a guy in the church named Bryan and he was like some sort of saint in the church. In his younger days, he was running from Brawely police officers, and when he was cornered he turned his gun on himself. It didn't kill him, but left him wheelchair bound. He was real arrogant and kind of rude. One day I was chosen to help him move to a house across the street from the church. He promised to hook us up with a bomb meal afterward. We busted our ass all day moving everything the guy owned. When we were done and exhausted, he phoned Domino's pizza and ordered a medium pizza for the four of us. Damn, these folks had no shame. But that was just to be expected in the home. I eventually got put on the lawn crew with Raul. We were required to mow, trim, edge, and anything else these church members would tell us to do. I guess if you donated enough money to the church, you were eligible for free lawn service from the New Creations slave pool. And these folks took full advantage of this shit. One day at this woman's home, we had completed her yard and we were loading up to go to the next saint's house. The woman came out and looked at her front porch. She called us back. She looked at me and said, "I want these spider webs removed from my entire porch. When you're done I want it to sparkle, do you understand?" I was thinking, "You better call Corky's Pest Control bitch." But instead I said, "Yes mame." As I was wiping off the light fixtures, she said, "And when you're done, mow my next door neighbor's lawn. His son washed my car last weekend." I said, "No problem." She said, "I know it's not a problem because it's your job young man." I just glared at her and went back to cleaning the webs. And of course, while I was doing it, Raul knocked out her neighbor's yard. That was my last day on lawn crew because my knee simply hurt too much.

On a beautiful Sunday morning, the church was hosting a guest speaker at Sunbeam Lake. Naturally, like all special events, we were required to be up at 5:00 am to set up the sound system, the chairs, the instruments, etc. for the affair. On this day, a gentleman named Rocco Morelli was speaking. Pastor Morelli had written a book entitled, "Forgetta Bout It (from Mafia to Ministry)" His story was simple, but powerful. He was a rising star in the Italian Mafia and was told to whack a thug named Big Tony. While he was riding with Big Tony to the spot where he was going to put him down, Rocco saw a sign on a Holiday Inn marque that announced a Christian revival that night. For some unknown reason, Rocco turned the car around and went into the meeting. Long story short, Pastor Morelli found Christ, let Big Tony off the hook, and he's been a ministering Man of God ever since. I sat there listening intently, but instead of being inspired, I was like...That's it? That's all it took? Man, you have no idea what loss is about. Well good for you. That's a terrible place to be, to hear an uplifting, positive, and redemptive story like Rocco's and the best I could do was think, "What do you know about loss?" The truth of the matter was that I would have loved to sit down with Pastor Morelli and share my plight at the current time, but it was so detailed, that it would take 2 hours and I was sure that he would come to the same conclusion that others had. Which was, sucks to be you, good luck with that. I hadn't found any hope yet, but I wasn't going to give up. I would still get depressed, especially when we would have Family Day. That was when guys in the home would invite their family members to spend a couple of hours with them in the Fellowship Hall of the church one Sunday of the month, after services. Each family would bring a dish and it would be pot luck style. Since I didn't have any family, I would just work the event, and serve the family members. What else did I have to do? But it hurt me intensely. But every time I began to get down, something would pull me up. Like one Sunday after church we were walking out of the auditorium, going to pick up the chairs in the gym, and I saw one of my players from Calexico High named Richie. He was walking with his girlfriend and I ran over and nudged him. He turned around and I just waved as I kept walking. He looked at me with this strange stare and waved back. For me, since we weren't allowed to talk to anyone, I felt like I got one over on them. I was going to let people know that I was here and I am coming back. That's not to say that I was any better off, I just had a new goal of not quitting. No matter what! I would still avoid certain things that were just too tough for me, like working at the IVC fireworks show. Man, this is where I would take my sons on the 4th of July to watch the fireworks every year. If I would have went there it would have been too emotional. So I volunteered to do some shit job at the home to avoid having to go there. As I sat there alone in the home, I got on my knees and said to God, "Father, you know that I've done my best here and you see both my physical and emotional pain. I know that it's through your divine spirit that I am given strength and power. Lord, please give me the power and the courage to leave this place. I'm not living, I'm only existing. I know you didn't place me on this earth to just exist. I believe it's time for me to leave here and all of it's insanity. Please guide me and give me discernment as to how I should make my exit from here. Heavenly Father, I put it in your hands to show me signs and lead me out of here in your time. In Jesus name I pray, Amen."

The next day I was placed on Moto by Pastor Tommie for not scrubbing the dining hall as well as he wanted me to do it. I had never been put on Moto for my entire 7 months there. Man, this was my sign from the Lord! It was time to go. Since I wasn't absolutely sure, I went with Ralph to the store to buy me some slacks for this performance that we were going to put on at the fairgrounds. Ralph picked out some pants that looked like Angel Flight's from back in the day and they were as thin as rice paper. Since they were only $4.00, I said, "Cool." I was pretty sure I wasn't going to wear them, but just in case I had to, I was covered. A guy named Tim, who was a former police chief in El Centro, would drop by the home often and bring ice cream for the brothers. He arrived this night and while we were eating the ice cream he said, "I can't wait until tomorrow night to watch you fellas perform and to eat some great food." I don't know how I knew, but I knew, that this was the final straw. I loved Tim, but no one was ever going to see me performing for this group ever again. Hell, the street was looking better than this pit of hell. That's really sad, but I felt exactly that way. Since I was now on Moto, I had to do the dishes for the guys that ate ice cream. Then I couldn't go to bed until an hour later than the other brothers. But when I went to bed, I thanked the Lord for guiding my steps. Since it was my last night there and I wasn't going to perform like a dancing monkey the following night, I smiled.

The following morning I woke up refreshed and packed my belongings and stored them in the closet. I was going to wait until after breakfast to leave. I had seen Tommie send guys on their way at all hours of the night with nothing to eat if they even mentioned leaving. After breakfast, I took off my Moto badge and threw it on the dresser. I picked up my bag and walked down the stairs. Raul stopped me and said, "Dude, where are you going?" I said, " I'm out of here." He said, "No. Eddie, what about your kids? Don't do it bro." I answered, "If I stay here I'll never see them. Take care bro." Other brothers tried to stop me and I just kept walking. I couldn't take one more hour in that oppressive dump. I stopped by the office and asked Eddie for my Bible and any money that I had left. He gave it to me and I walked out of that joint for the first time in 7 months, without permission. I didn't know where I was going or what I was going to do, but I knew the Lord had my back. Or at least I thought so. As I smelled the morning air, I smiled.

Now what? I had no clue. I just knew that I had served a month over my required time at the home and I was going to do nothing but go further down if I stayed. I went to the pay phone down the street and called my Dad. Once again, he didn't accept my collect call. Oh well. I looked in the envelope that Eddie gave me and it had $7.00. Before I left Ralph, told me that Tommie was on the phone with probation to notify them that I had left the home. I didn't know what that meant but I figured I needed to stay out of sight from the authorities. In retrospect, I don't know why I was so paranoid, but I was. I walked over two blocks and went to the bus station. From my previous trip to IVC, I knew there was nothing for me there so I bought a bus ticket to Calexico, the only other place I knew. I hopped on the bus to Calexico with my head spinning. When I got there, I got off the bus and walked about 2 miles to the maple tree across the street from the boys elementary school (the one I would pick them up at everyday). When I got there I rested for a minute and then pulled my clothes out of my bag. Yeah, all 3 t-shirts and my one pair of sweats. I had pulled them out of the washer when I packed and they were still wet. So I laid them out in the sun to dry. I sat there under the tree and it hit me. This was the tree that I picked my boys up everyday. As I sat there I began to cry. How in the world did I get here? What did I do to lose everything? I just sat there for the whole day. When the sun started to go down I walked up the street to the Jack in the Box and sat there. It would be nightfall soon, so I had to do something quick. Since I had no choice, I asked this kid if I could use his phone. I called Ralph's phone and he answered. I said, "Ralph, this is Coach. I made a big mistake. Can you come pick me up in Calexico?" He said, " I would, but we're just leaving the fairgrounds." Just then, Tommie got on the phone and said, "Richey, you're not coming back to the home. You made a big boy decision this morning and now you have some big boy consequences." I pleaded with him and he just kept saying no. Ralph got back on the phone and said, "Try to get back to the home tomorrow." I said, "What am I going to do tonight?" He said, "It's warm, it won't kill you to sleep outside one night." I said, "OK." And hung up. I went back under the tree and laid down. I used my bag for a pillow and I went to sleep. I didn't sleep very well because I kept waking up thinking a cop was rolling up every time I heard a car. In the morning I walked back up to the store. I asked a guy, getting gas, if he was going to El Centro and he said he was. I asked him for a ride and he said he would. He dropped me off at the 4th street off ramp. I walked from there the three miles to the home. I just sat outside the home, because I didn't know of any place else to go. A guy named Ed pulled up to the curb. I had gotten to know Ed pretty good because he was studying for the same degree that I had in Alcohol & Drug Studies, and we would chat often. It was Saturday, so he was there to do his internship for his course study. We talked, and after I told him what happened, he offered to put me up in a Motel 6 for the night, and hopefully Tommie would change his mind the following day after church. I accepted his offer and he drove me over to the motel. I got all checked in and Ed left. It was weird, I hadn't watched T.V. in 7 months and here I was watching T.V. I took the longest shower that I've ever taken in my life and I laid down and went to sleep. Since I never slept good in the home, I slept until the following morning. I got up and took another shower. I got dressed in my sweats and a t-shirt. I walked to Southwest High for church. It was strange to be able to wear casual clothes and sit wherever I wanted (not with the goon squad of New Creations). After the service I talked to Ralph and he said it was

OK with him for me to return to the home. But I had to talk to Tommie. I walked up to Tommie and he just said, "Absolutely not, you're not coming back." I went over to Tim and talked to him. Tim said he would be glad to put me up at the Motel 6 for another night. Just then, Tommie walked over and said, "Tim, do not help that man in any way." I thought, "How does this concern you in the least asshole?" Tim said, "I'm sorry Eddie but he's the boss." Again I thought, " The boss of who?" Derek came over, after seeing what happened and said, "Eddie, here's my number, call me in about 30 minutes and since I'm going to San Diego today I'll give you a ride." I told him OK and I started walking to the 7/11 store. I called Derek for the rest of the day and he never answered. When it got dark, I walked down to El Centro Regional Hospital and went into the emergency room waiting area. I stayed in the ER most of the night pretending that I was waiting for someone. At about 1:00 am I went in the bathroom and fell asleep in a stall. In the morning I washed my face in the sink and walked out of the hospital. I figured I would do what I could to get up to the Probation Dept. to check in with them. I walked up to the 7/11 store and saw a guy that was in the New Creations home for a little while. His name was Robert and he was Pastor Walt's brother in law. We talked for a minute and he offered to buy me a hot dog. As I ate the hot dog he asked me what I was going to do. I told him that I needed to get to the Probation Dept. He said he would give me a ride, so off we went. Robert dropped me off at probation. I went in and met my probation officer, Liz, and she schooled me on what was expected. I assured her that I wouldn't be any trouble and I left. Now what? I remembered that a guy named Gilbert once told me about another Men's home named Heritage House. I looked it up in the phone book, got the address, and I walked down the road to check it out.

By the way, Pastor Tommie was forced to resign after he was caught, red handed, misusing the food stamp cards. When I heard that, I laughed and smiled.

I walked to the Heritage building in El Centro which was about 5 miles away. When I got there all the doors were locked and the gates were closed. I waited for about 2 hours, but since the sun was going down, I had to start thinking about where I was going to sleep. I remembered that a friend of mine named Martin worked at a place that people who had DUI's went to get their driver's licenses' back. Martin and I were in a lot of classes together at IVC. I walked in the door and Martin greeted me with a hug. I sat down and told him everything that had happened and he was real disappointed. I eventually would see

that look a lot. He said, "Ed, let's go to an AA meeting down the street." I said, "Sure." We went to the meeting and it was pretty much like every meeting I had ever been to. Only this time, when the meeting was over, I was faced with the fact that I had nowhere to go. We stood out in the night air and talked for a while. Martin said, "Where are you going to go?" I replied, " I don't know bro. I really don't have a clue." He reached into his pocket and pulled out $14.00 and handed it to me. He said, "That's all I have bro." I thanked him, gave him a hug, and walked down the street. I went to a store and bought Copenhagen and got 2 dollars in quarters. I went to a pay phone and phoned my Dad. I figured if it wasn't a collect call he might answer. Unfortunately, he didn't answer and I hung up. I felt so alone and wondered if I had what it takes to live on the streets. Homeless people are very cunning and resourceful. I walked around the corner and saw a sign that read Imperial Valley Ministries. I walked in and it was pitch black. A guy walked towards me with a flashlight and asked me, "Can I help you?" I said, "I need a place to stay because I'm homeless and have nowhere to go." He took my bag and led me to a room that smelled so funky that I didn't even want to breathe. He said I could take the top bunk. He said, "I'll talk to you in the morning, go to sleep." I crawled up into the bunk and fell fast asleep. I was so mentally, physically, emotionally, and spiritually exhausted. At about 5:00 in the morning I was awoken by thundering yelling and clapping. All the brothers in the home were dancing around in the next room like they were possessed. They were speaking in tongues and screaming. It was scary at first. I just laid in the bed and wondered, once again, how in the hell did I get here? When their prayer time ended it got immediately quiet. A guy named Panda, I bullshit you not the guy introduced himself as Panda, came in the room and handed me some papers. I knew I didn't want to stay in this place but I didn't have a choice. Panda asked me for my I.D and I told him that I didn't have one. He asked for the papers back and he said, "We can't admit you into the home without some form of I.D" I said, "OK, where's my bag?" He took me outside and unlocked a storage container. I picked up my bag, thanked him, and walked down Main Street. Man, that place was a trip, but I figured it wasn't in God's plan for me to stay there. At least I didn't have to sleep in the streets so I smiled.
I walked back to the Heritage building and sat down. I just sat there and prayed. I said, "Lord, I know you have a plan and it's all for my own good. I praise you with all of my heart and have faith, that in your time, you will pull me out of this pit. Father send me where you want

me to be and I will go and serve you to the best of my ability. Use me as your hands and feet here on earth. Please heal my knee and make me strong and capable. Jesus, you know how difficult it can be here on earth, I invoke your mighty name to petition to our Father on my behalf. I need somewhere to go. Please help me. In Jesus precious name I pray, Amen." About 10 minutes later, a truck drove up and stopped in from of the building. A Mexican guy got out and asked me if I wanted to come into the Heritage home. I said yes and he grabbed my bag and threw it into the bed of the truck. We drove to this deserted house out in the middle of nowhere. It was on 2 acres of land and looked like it had been abandoned long ago. It was bordered by a chain link fence that was locked. The guy, Mario, got out of the truck and unlocked the gate. We drove in and stopped along side a patio. Mario took me into the house and introduced me to a dude named brother Mike. The house was filthy and was kind of spooky. I talked to Mike, who was the home director, for a while and he showed me to my room. The room was tiny and stunk like shit. There were 3 beds crammed in there so you could hardly walk around. Mike told me that I could put my stuff in this metal cabinet that was located in the corner of the room. Mike said he had some things to do, and for me to just relax. After he left, I unpacked my bag and stored my clothes away. It's not like I had that much anyway. At that point, I had one pair of shorts, three t-shirts, four pairs of socks, one pair of underwear, and an IVC windbreaker. That's it! When I was finished I walked outside and looked around. The place was basically a landfill. They didn't have trash pick up, they just took the trash out to the exterior of the property and dumped it. The trash pile was about 30 yards long and 9 feet high. There were rats in there as big as poodles. Most of the grounds were dirt so when the wind blew it created one hell of a dust storm. In the backyard, there was an empty swimming pool filled with trash and debris. I stood there in the backyard, looked up, and said, "Lord, I know that you have my best interest in mind, and that this is part of my journey but please don't let me rot here."

Heritage Family Fellowship is run by Pastor Frank, an ex-heroin addict, gang banger, and con man. He is another one of those guys that hustles for the Lord. Everything is about him and how he can make money for himself. So much so, that after I was there three days, the city came and turned off all of the gas and electric for non payment. And it was never turned back on the entire time I stayed there. The same day that they cut off the power, DEA officers raided the home. They brought drug-sniffing dogs and everything. I had no idea what was going on. They searched the entire house, but luckily they came up with nothing. I was in shock! Here I was trying to serve God and get my life in order, and I could possibly get caught up in a drug sting. When the pastor got word of the raid he was livid. When the gas & electric guys left after turning off all the utilities, they left the front gate unlocked. It was made clear to everyone in the home that the gate was to remain locked at all times. He ripped into the dude that was left in charge of the home. I guess if the gate is locked, the authorities can't enter the property without a search warrant. I don't know that to be a fact, but that is what I was told. The place was a fuckin joke. My probation officer, Liz, came to the home one day and I gave her the tour. I showed her the fire pit where we took buckets of canal water and heated it up to take a shower. Yep, we heated up a bucket of mosquito infested canal water, then carried it into the bathroom, and used a cup to wash off with. I showed her the empty refrigerator that was useless because we had no electricity. Before Liz left, she walked me to her car and said, "Eddie, I don't know how you're going to do it, but you have to get out of here." I said, "Well, the fact that I don't have any family down here in the Valley makes it impossible. Not to mention that I still have to complete 10 days of community service for the DUI, and I don't even have the $100.00 to apply for the community service. That's one reason I came here, because I was told that I would be able to find a job and earn the 100 bucks. And every time I phone my Dad, he just hangs up on me or doesn't answer at all." She looked me square in the eye and said, " Get the money somehow, do the community service, and I'll give you clearance to go wherever you want. I know you're not a threat, so I won't have any reservations about letting you go. But the bottom line is that this place is shady as hell and I don't want to see you get caught up in any bullshit." She drove off and I had my goal right in front of me.

I went into the house and dug around in the closet in my room. I found a pair of slacks that fit me, a white dress shirt that was stained but it would have to do, a tie, and some old scuffed up dress shoes. These would be my church clothes. We had church every Wednesday and Sunday at the building down in El Centro. We would all pile in to Mike's truck and head down there. It was a Pentecostal Church and had about 15 members. They were burnt out druggies from the neighborhood. Frank would drive up, well actually he didn't drive because he didn't have a driver's license, but his wife would drive up and park in front of the building. He would get out like he was the President in his cheap suit, which he thought was the shit. He would walk in and start straightening the chairs and spraying air freshener. He would do his sermon in Spanish, which left me completely lost. In an hour's sermon, he did half on different verses, but you could bet your ass that the other half would be completely devoted to one verse. That verse was Malachi 3:8 which states, "Will a man rob God? Yet you rob me." (NIV) He was so damn phony in trying to make his tiny flock feel guilty for not tithing more. It was fucking sickening because he would preach that part in English and Spanish to make sure no change was left behind. One time, he had his pastor, a pimp-looking hustler from Los Angeles come preach at his shack. This guy was more glossy than Frank. The pimp's wife was a 300 lb. blob named Mama Jo Ann. She got up at the end of the service and claimed that the Lord just put it on her heart that we should take up a collection to buy pastor Frank and his wife a car. I couldn't believe what I was hearing. Don't these motherfuckers have any shame? Frank jumped up to the pulpit and started urging people to make a pledge towards the car. He said, "I have gold pledge envelopes for you saints that want to contribute $1000.00, silver pledge envelopes for you that want to give $500.00, and bronze envelopes for those who are willing to donate $100.00 to this worthy cause. Know that you will be blessed by your donation one hundred fold. Mama Jo Ann is a woman of God, so if He put it on her heart you know that it is divinely inspired. You don't want your pastor driving around town in a Chevy Blazer. Don't you want to see your pastor driving a top of the line vehicle? Then you'll be proud to say that's my pastor." It was the biggest crock of shit I've ever heard! I don't know how he did it with a straight face. And the capper was when people began shouting, "I'll take a silver envelope.", or "I'll take 2 bronze envelopes.", Etc. And everyone would clap. Needless to say, that scumbag never got no damn car. But you can best believe that if anyone did give him any money, he didn't offer to give it back. That's just how the guy was. I was sitting outside one day next to Frank while I was eating my bologna burrito and he said to me, "Coach, do you notice anything different about these jeans I'm wearing?" I said, "No." He said, "I have all of my jeans tailored so that they pull all of the original hems out and re-sew them with this special braid thread. Doesn't it look better?" I said, " Absolutely, what are those Wrangler's ?" He said, "I don't know but they are very expensive." He didn't even realize I was busting on him. I just looked down and smiled.

Things at Heritage were comical but most of it was disturbing. Most of the guys that were in the home were drug addicts. One night I woke up to see Mario in the bed beside mine shooting heroin. It was crazy, this was supposed to be a Christian Men's Home, and here I was witnessing something that I had never seen in the streets. To watch someone who is high on heroin is disgusting. I used to wonder why Mario would volunteer to go sleep at the church. Sleeping at the church was brutal. I guess they had some break ins in the past, so two guys from the home would be required to sleep there every night. We had to take our blanket and pillow and clean the church. Then we slept on the cold floor. But Mario loved it because he could have his connection drop off his drugs and he could party all night.

It was around Christmas time of 2010. I volunteered to work at the San Diego Food Bank. It was my job to pack Christmas gifts for needy children. I had a list that had the kid's last name, how many kid's were in the home, and if they were boys or girls. I would pick out toys that were appropriate for the children, put them in a plastic bag, and label the bag with their last name. I really felt like I was doing something useful and I realized it had been such a long time since I felt that way. I started wondering what my kids would be receiving for Christmas. I thought about what they must be going through not having their Dad there on Christmas morning. They were the ones that would really suffer this holiday season. They had to be wondering where I was and why I didn't at least call. The thought hurt so much. A guy named Jim came in to pick up the bags and he said, "Hey Coach, do you have any kids?" I said, "Yes, I have three boys, but one is grown." He said, "Go ahead and make up a bag for them and I'll come back to get it when I store these." I said, "Thanks Jim, but my ex-wife has a restraining order against me and I'm to have no contact with her or my sons." He said, "That sucks dude." I agreed and went back to loading the bags with toys.

My best friend in the Heritage house was a brother named DJ who was from East San Diego. DJ was an ex-Crip from 40's. He had a drinking problem and had come to the Valley to get his life straightened out. He initially went to Imperial Valley Ministries for a year. The fact that he was African American eventually got him kicked out of there. Like I've mentioned before, those Mexicans are some of the most racist motherfuckers you'll find anywhere. I guarantee if they spent one hour in our neighborhood, they would change their tune real quick. But that's just how they are, get them in the majority and they become real hard asses. So DJ showed up at Heritage shortly after I did. We became fast friends and volunteered to do fund raising. See, Frank or Mike would take the brother's food stamp cards and go to Smart &

Final each morning and purchase boxes of candy that held 30 bars. The box cost $15.00 and we would sell them for $1.00 apiece for a profit of $15.00, if we sold out (and we always did). DJ and I would roam around El Centro with our box of candy, sometimes 15 miles in a day, and ask anyone and everyone if they would like to make a donation to the church. It was funny when people would say, "What church?" and we would reply, "Heritage Church" and they would say, " Is that Frank's church?" we would say, "Yes" and they would say, "I wouldn't give that phony con man a dime!" DJ and I would walk away chuckling. Because we knew that Frank was full of shit. The profit each day of $15.00 would go directly into the pocket of his cheap ass jeans. Basically, it was a way to turn food stamp vouchers into cash, plain and simple. It sure wasn't used to feed us. He used our food stamp cards to buy food for his family at home. Straight scandalous! But like I said, the dude had no shame, period. From my personal experience, you have to have done time in prison to become a pastor these days. Frank had been to prison and I once heard him say, "That's how we used to rape the fish up in Soladad prison." Now this is a man of God? I had no respect for that asshole. So me and DJ would hustle the candy each day and usually we would have more than the $30.00 that Frank demanded. Brother Mike told us to keep what ever we collected over $30.00. We would come away with about $3.00 each. Since we didn't eat hardly anything at the home, we would stop at In N Out Burger and eat a hamburger before we went home. DJ really needed to eat well because he had diabetes, high blood pressure, he was over weight, and had a heart condition. With my bad knee, we looked like a pair walking down the street. Frank was even more racist than any of those other fools. DJ's uncle died and he had his brother come get him to take him back to San Diego for his funeral. When DJ's brother got there to pick him up, Frank walked up to the car and began telling him how good a man DJ was and how he didn't see color. He went on and on about how non-racist he was that it became embarrassing. The guy was a clown, period. In my experience, if you're not a racist, you never have to tell someone that you're not racist. And you certainly don't start a conversation by saying you're not racist. That was the longest week I ever had, because with DJ gone, I had to sell 2 boxes of candy instead of one. When DJ returned I was overjoyed. I told him about how I had started to stand out in front of the Rite-Aid store in El Centro, and sold the candy from there, instead of walking all over town. Neither of us should have to walk 15 miles a day with my bad knee and his sore feet. So that's what we started to do. We would post up, come rain or shine, out in front of Rite-Aid. It was difficult because, just speaking for myself, I looked like a bum. The canal water showers didn't do shit and my clothes were really ragged. You could feel some people thought we were disgusting by their looks. It was strange because the one thing that I resented about New Creations was the rule that we couldn't talk to anyone while outside of the house. Now I could talk to people I knew, but I would duck if I saw someone I knew. I had lost 45 lbs., I was dressed like a bum, and I stunk. I didn't want anyone seeing me like that.

On Christmas Eve, DJ got the idea to take the bus to Calexico to sell the candy. We were really running dry at Rite-Aid. So I agreed, even though I was deathly afraid of Mark and Robert seeing me like that. Who wants to know their Dad is a homeless bum? But I went anyway. We stood outside of the Food for Less grocery store in Calexico. We had been there 2 hours or so and I saw him...Mitz' Dad coming out of the store. I hadn't seen or heard from the boys in 9 months. I told DJ to go ask him how my sons were doing. DJ walked up to him and said, " Eddie wanted me to ask you how his sons are doing?" That cold-hearted snake said, "They're doing fine without him. I hope they never see him again." When DJ returned and told me what he said, I put down the candy and started walking toward him. Something inside me told me to hold my peace and let the Lord fight my battle. I stopped and went back and grabbed my candy box. It was at that moment that I realized I could never take another man's life. Because I had so much rage, resentment, and hurt at the time that I could have beat that wet back to death. Hell, what did I have to lose? I was already just existing. I had no hope for the future and to tell you the truth, I was suicidal most of the time. Back at the home, I would often go into this abandoned house and make a noose to hang myself with. A couple of times I slid it over my head and pull it tight on my throat. One time I actually stepped off the chair and it felt like me eyes were going to pop out of my head. But like every other time I had been to that point, I changed my mind. I was just going to have to see this thing through. Maybe, just maybe, God would lift me out of this hellish pit. I didn't know how, but I had faith that He would. And that's what faith is, Belief in the Unseen!

Our morning prayers were a joke. Everyone woke up at 5:30 am and met in the living room. This Pentecostal bullshit was for the birds. The ones that claimed to speak in tongues were a riot. They would shout, "Shalabofrey", and carry on like mental patients. Every time Frank would pray hard he would say Shalabofrey. His wife, the pastora, would yell Shalabofrey. So all of these morons would say that stupid shit. It's my understanding that speaking in tongues is guided by the Holy Spirit and it's individualized to you only. This wasn't speaking in tongues, this was chanting. And if you're chanting, you should at least know what the hell Shalabofrey means. Don't get me wrong, I believe in speaking in tongues, but these folks were nothing but actors. And poor ones at that!

Memorial Day came and we were looking forward to a day off. Because I didn't only sell candy during the day, I was responsible for shoveling up all the dog shit on the property. So this day off would be a nice break. We were told to relax and then we would drive down to a park over on the east side of El Centro for a picnic. Me and DJ were in our room when Mike called us to go see the pastor. We walked outside and there stood Frank with two boxes of candy. He said, "DJ and Coach, start walking to the park on the east side and sell these candies on your way." The park was about 5 miles away. Everyone else in the home was enjoying their day off and were going to get a ride to the park. That's right, all the Mexicans were going to be driven to the park, and the black dude and the white dude would walk while selling candy. That son of a bitch was getting on my last nerve! But we did it. When we arrived at the park, we waited for the rest of the guys. When they showed we helped unload the truck and set up for the picnic. Like I mentioned before, Frank used the food stamp cards for his own home, but on this day he would be generous and buy us a few chicken legs and some coleslaw. As we ate, some of the guys were playing softball. I didn't participate because my knee hurt so bad from making the walk there. Some other people were playing on an adjacent field. Frank got this bullhorn and challenged them to a game. He starts running his mouth about how we have the IVC Coach on our side. I told him I didn't want to play because my knee was real bad. He turned around and said, "You're playing or you can find somewhere else to live." I said, "Frank, I can hardly walk." He said, "Pray it away Coach, now get out there." I was fuckin pissed! I played but from that point on I knew I had to get out of that place. I couldn't take much more of this prick. If I would have had anywhere else to go, I would have knocked his ugly ass out.

The food situation became a real problem. Frank would get donations from the San Diego Food Bank every 2 weeks for the home. He claimed he was running a Christian Outreach program for men down on their luck and also a rehab for those addicted to drugs or alcohol.

Yes, the dudes here were certainly addicts, but it damn sure wasn't a rehab. All day guys in the home were either chasing a fix or fixing. But anyway, when the Food Bank would drop off the donation, Frank would load anything decent into his Blazer to take home to his family. And get this, the rest would be taken to the church to pass out to church members. We would often have a dozen eggs, a pack of bologna, and some tortillas to make breakfast burritos, between 13 people. It was outrageous how heartless that bastard was.

There were at least 10 dogs on the property. Most of them were pit bulls. I came home one day from selling candy. And this guy comes up to me and says, "We have a Judas dog Coach." I said, "Where?" He pointed out towards the back yard. In the distance I could see something hanging from one of the dog cages. I walked the hundred yards out there, and I couldn't believe what I saw. One of the pit bulls had jumped over the fence and hung himself. He was just hanging there, I went and got a knife and cut the heavy leash. He dropped with a thud. Who in their right mind would chain up an animal when he's in a locked cage? These stupid idiots, that's who. I went in the house and asked Mike what I should do with him, call Animal Control or what? He said, without blinking an eye, "No, just put him in a wheel barrow and dump him in the trash pile." I couldn't believe it, but I did it. I looked down at that poor dog and said, " I'm sorry buddy. I hope you're in a better place. But I guarantee, they ain't tossing me in this pile. I'm gonna get out."

There was this little drifter named Will and he was pretty resourceful. We were talking one night and I was telling him that I really needed to get my Medi-Cal card and my food stamp card. I told him that my problem was that I didn't have any form of I.D. He said, "That's no problem. Do you know your Social Security number?" I said, "Yes, of course." He said, "Cool, we'll just go to the Social Security office tomorrow and get you a new card. That's all you need." I said, "Alright." So the next day we walked to the office and I got a temporary SS card. I was able to do this because by selling the candy I could walk around town and sell it anywhere. So I chose to sell in the Social Security parking lot. I was really overjoyed, because at New Creations I was told that I couldn't get any aid without a picture I.D. That was total bullshit. But since you couldn't leave the home, there was no way to research things like that on your own. I went to the Social Services offices and got my Medi-Cal and a food stamp cards. Once I activated the food stamp card I had $200.00 in my account. I hadn't had any sort of real meal in 3 months, if you don't count the In

N Out burgers, so I walked over to Albertson's grocery store and bought a cooked whole chicken and an apple pie. I sat on the side of the store and ate the entire chicken along with the pie. I was stuffed. I still didn't have a picture I.D, but this was a good start to becoming a person again.

A new kid came into the home named Pete. Pete was a spoiled kid and knew how to hustle his parents. He only lasted 2 days in New Creations because he smoked, did drugs, and was very rebellious. He actually got put on Moto the first day he was there. They booted him after 2 days. So Pete could pick up his phone, call one of his parents, and he would have whatever he wanted to eat at the front gate in 30 minutes. He would go out in his mom's car, score drugs and cigarettes, and come right back to the home. He was set. He would constantly get caught for smoking, but he would never face any discipline because his parents would make sizable donations to Frank's so-called church. He would even go behind one of shacks out back and fire up his meth pipe. This kid wasn't changing for no one. He was talented though, he could play the guitar as well as I've ever heard anyone and he raced cars professionally. He just couldn't leave the crystal alone. So as time went along me, Pete, DJ, and Beto became good friends. With Pete on our side, we didn't have to sit on another dude's lap on our way to church. Pete would just call his mother Debbie and we would ride to church in style, and she would treat us all to Jack in the Box. The piece of shit vatos in the home would try to mooch our food but we just told them to kick rocks. We were the four outcasts in the home because me and Pete were white, DJ was black, and Beto was clean and sober and he didn't want any of that drug shit around him. We ate decent food that Debbie would bring over, we went to her house to take showers, and we did our laundry there too. The guys in the home that didn't have family had to wash their clothes in one of the shower buckets, well they actually just soaked their clothes in heated up canal water. Beto worked at the Food Bank every day so we were never at a loss for snacks. Me and DJ began storing our candies that were left over in drawers, so we brought that to the party. So it became one big hustle. I would go to one of the vatos and say, "I'll give you a Snickers for a razor." And they would say, "Hell yeah." Since we had no electricity it was totally dark in the home when the sun went down. If Debbie brought over pizza I would light my candle and walk through the home trying to trade two slices of pizza for someone's flashlight. If they didn't agree to the trade, I would put them on candy restriction. That meant I would no longer trade my candy with them no matter what they offered. The barter system works real good when you're dealing with dudes that are just out of prison. They understand and respect the system. Unlike New Creations, where most of the brothers are just out of county jail, Heritage was for guys that just got released from doing considerable time in the pen. It was common place in Heritage to see a guy wearing an ankle monitor. You never knew what those guys did to get that ankle jewelry but you knew it wasn't good. They didn't accept men with monitors in New Creations because you couldn't work your ass off for them with one on. Now, we were seeing guys leave Heritage that had monitors because we didn't have any electricity, so they couldn't charge their monitors. That was a fuckin joke. The court would sentence a man to 6 months or a year to the Heritage home with an ankle monitor, and when he would get there and learn he couldn't charge his monitor, he would freak. He would have to call his PO and the PO would jump Frank or Mike's ass for not disclosing that information when he dropped him off. So after a while, the court knew that the Heritage house was a shady operation. While watching money grubbing Frank get his ass chewed, I smiled.

Most of the brothers had family except DJ and I. On Christmas Eve of 2010 everyone in the house went to visit their families. Me and DJ were left alone in the house. We just laid in our bunks and I don't remember who brought up the subject, but we began to sing Motown and R&B songs. We went on for hours. This was a nice change because we weren't allowed to go around singing any secular songs or anything that wasn't considered Christian music. Personally, I hated the music that we sang in church. It was all so corny. It was hard to sing "I've Got Satan Under My Feet.", When in actuality, Satan had me in a rear naked choke hold and he was squeezing the life out of me. I had fallen into such a depressive pit, with no conceivable way out, that I was suffering through a soul sickness that was so severe that I really didn't want to live anymore. It's a terrible place to be! I lived in a constant state of self-loathing, guilt, shame, and hopelessness. I had no more tears left, so I just walked around in a catatonic state. I hated myself for all the mistakes I had made. When you can't get along with yourself, it's impossible to get along with others. So I just stayed to myself (except for DJ) and worried. See, you reflect outside what you feel on the inside. And I was reflecting defeat to everyone I came in contact with. It wasn't like anyone cared, and I don't blame them, because who wants to be around a perpetually depressed and withdrawn person? So at the time, I spent most of my free time in my bunk looking up at the ceiling. My knee had become so painful that the only thing that helped was lying down. Since I now had medical insurance, I went to the clinic by the home and had my knee checked out. They did an x-ray and diagnosed it as a strain. I knew it was more because as an athlete, I know my body, and no strain would have lasted this long. I was going on a year and a half. The doctor at the clinic gave me Tylenol for my knee and Prozac for my depression. I began taking the medications as prescribed, but they didn't relieve my knee pain or the depression. I did receive some good news. I don't know how, but my brother got the cell number to one of the guys in the home. He called one night and asked how I was doing. I told him not too well. He asked if I needed anything and I told him that he could really help me if he would send me a money order for $100.00, so I could sign up for my community service through Cal-Trans. He agreed to do it and I gave him the home's address. When I received the money order I went down to the Cal-Trans office and signed up. For the next 10 days I woke up at 4:30 am, washed off the best I could with the freezing canal water and got dressed. I walked the 4 miles to the Cal-Trans yard and waited for them to open. I picked up trash along the highway and returned to the yard. Then I walked back to the home. After I completed the 10 days, I walked to the courthouse and had myself put on the calendar. The public defender came over and I gave him my certificate of completion. Right then court was in session and the Judge took his seat on the bench. It wasn't just any Judge, it was Bill. He looked down at me and smiled. He probably had no idea it was me because the case said Ralph Richey and he knew me as Eddie Richey. The public defender showed the prosecutor my certificate and he approved it. Then they passed it to Bill. He looked it over and said, "OK Eddie, I mean Mr. Richey, you have completed what was required. Have a nice day." I walked to the door at the back of the courtroom and looked back, Bill just winked, and I was on my way. I felt good because with that out of the way, I just needed a place to go and I could get the hell out of the Imperial Valley. A place I should have never been in the first place.

Nothing or no one could help me. I had no choice but to turn to God for relief. The Lord promises to bring us out of every storm. And He promises to bring you out better than you were before. I believed He would, but I didn't have much faith in myself, that I could hold on while He moved in my life. As I laid in my bunk one afternoon, I closed my eyes, and prayed, "Father, I invite Jesus and the Holy Spirit to be present right now. Lord, my life is so full of unhappiness, depression, heartache, and worthlessness. For all of the mistakes I've made in my life, especially the ones that offended you, I humbly ask for your forgiveness. Please give me discernment in regards to your word and my life in general. You know that I've placed my entire life in your hands and that I'm a willing servant to you for whatever purpose you see fit. I don't feel like I'm doing anything to bring glory to your name and I feel like I'm the last person on earth to represent you to others. But I am here, and I ask that you give me knowledge of your will and the power to carry it out. You know that I have tremendous faith in you, your power, your grace, your mercy, and your peace. I just need to be shown those blessings because I don't know that I can go on, or even want to go on, because this place is soul robbing. Don't let this home rob me of my love and faith in you. Show me the way out and set me on a path to peace. I love you and honor you all the days of my life. In Jesus holy name I pray, Amen." I laid there with my eyes still closed and meditated on the mercy of God. Then, out of nowhere, I saw this vision of Jesus that shocked me so intensely that I sat up and hit my head on the upper bunk. After checking to see if I was bleeding (I wasn't) I laid back down. I laid there for a few moments, then for the first time in my life, Jesus spoke to me audibly. He said, "My son, what you are facing is not a test from me. I'm here and I will never leave you. You are never alone. The evil one is the one that is bringing you pain. Stay faithful and true to me and I will fight your battle for you. I know your pain and the trials that are causing them. Do not fear, for I will defeat them for you. Trust what I say to you my son because you have a bright future and you will be restored. You have not been left out. Endure the storm that is taking up so much of your time and energy. Don't wait for the storm to calm to start living your life in me. Live now and know that your life is in my hands, now and forever. Be confident that I will surely do what I say. Rest and I will fill you with the hope that you seek. Receive this my son." I just laid there stunned. Nothing had changed on the outside or in my surroundings, but I knew everything was going to work out in His time. I got down on my knees and praised God, as I smiled.

Have you ever stepped in dog crap but you didn't know that you did? Soon afterwords though, you get a whiff of the veil smell and it's then, and only then, that you begin checking the soles of your shoes to see if the foul smell is coming from you. Well, that's where I was. Except the smell was the voice of truth. I knew that I had been blessed with pure truth and it wasn't going away. I had to search out how I could fulfill my destiny. Jesus had it all mapped out for me and now I just had to keep my eyes and ears open to His guidance. This was no time to be lazy or unaware of the blessings that He would surely show me. Now, don't be mistaken that I liked my present place of residence or the people I was living with, but I knew deep in my heart that I wouldn't be there forever. That was such a relief. I remembered how I thought I was going to be a lifer at New Creations, but that didn't happen. I believe that life is nothing more than endless waves of transformation. I saw my predicament as it was. As far as these two Men's homes were concerned, they were just two waves that sucked. I figured that the next wave would surely come and I would ride it no matter if it was good or bad. The Lord had promised me restoration and I believed Him without reservation. I made a promise to myself that I would take care of myself first. Because if I couldn't take care of myself, there would be no way I could help someone else. And I knew the Lord would one day use me in a mighty way. So instead of walking 10 or so miles each day to sell the candy, I went to this truck stop that was just around the corner of the house. I got to know everyone there and they allowed me to solicit on their property. I would sit at a table in front of the store and read my Bible. When a trucker would come out or in to the store, I would ask them if they wanted to make a donation to the church. This really helped my knee a lot. Plus, I had some of the best conversations with these truckers from across the nation. Often times they would make sizable donations and once I reached the $30.00 that I was required to turn in, then I would give the rest to the homeless people that hung around the truck stop. It felt so good to be helping others instead of begging and taking. I didn't need that burger at the end of the day because I knew my blessing was right around the corner. One time I was talking to this Christian trucker and he was so inspired that I would sit out there all day promoting the word of God, that he took my name and address and promised to send me some literature about Christ that I could pass out at the truck stop. A couple of weeks later a huge box arrived that was addressed to me. I had no idea what it could be, so I took it into my room and opened it. All the scumbag vultures in the home stood around in the doorway to see if it was anything they could steal or beg for. When I got the box opened, it was filled with little New Testament Bibles, Cd's, and tracks. The vultures scrammed when they saw what it was. That trucker was true to his word and I appreciated it. I wrote him a thank you letter. I wish I would have kept his name and address, but it got misplaced in that filthy home. I put as many of the Bibles in my backpack that I could fit and tossed the tracks in the trash. In my opinion, the tracks are nothing more than propaganda to discount different religions. Personally, I don't believe that every Jew, Mormon, Catholic, etc. is doomed to eternal damnation. But anyway, from then on when I went to the truck stop and would have a conversation with someone about Christ, I would give them a little Bible. I didn't push it on anyone, but if during our conversation they expressed an interest in the word of God, I gave them the New Testament. On a bright sunny Saturday afternoon I was walking to the truck stop and Jim (the IVC baseball coach) drove by. I almost turned like I normally did when I saw someone I knew, but I didn't. Jim had been too good a friend to me to not at least let him know I was still alive. I actually waved. He turned around and got out of his car. He hugged me and asked if I needed a ride. We were right across the street from the truck stop but I said I would ride with him anyway. We hadn't talked since I left his office to go to New Creations. I gave him the lowdown on how my Dad had rejected me, Mitz' restraining order which included the boys, and how miserable the conditions were at the Heritage home. He drove by the house and he saw that I wasn't exaggerating. He pulled over and I said, "Jim, I'm done. My life seems to be finished. I have faith in the Lord's plan but I don't think I'm able to wait much longer." He said, "Well, let's look at this, you can't call your Dad, you can't call Mitz, and the home is brutal." I know that he was thinking the same thing I was because I saw it in his eyes. That look of sadness and sorrow because there was nothing he could do. He finally said, "Just stick it out and something will change. A door will open and you'll be fine." He dropped me off at the truck stop and drove off. I felt like such a loser because I just depressed my good friend because of my predicament. I wanted to cry but I had no tears left.

It was obvious to me that I needed to leave Heritage and it's drug den. I had learned a lot about drug addicts (certainly more than I ever learned in my Alcohol & Drug Studies classes at IVC) and I was absolutely sure that I didn't want to work in that field. I had previously been under the impression that I would be able to sell addicts on the benefits of sobriety and encourage them to work the 12 Steps that led to sobriety if they would work them. I figured once they were on board, I would just have to encourage them and guide them towards a better life. Fact is, most addicts don't want to stop even if it means jails, institutions, and death. They will beg, borrow, and steal to achieve their goal of getting high. And it's always their goal! I'm not saying that no one ever recovers, I'm just saying they are few and far between. And as a baseball player, I have a real respect for averages.

Batting in the low hundreds isn't my cup of tea.

Frank came to the home one Saturday with a huge truck. I learned that someone had complained about the huge trash pile on the property. As I said, the pile was at least 30 yards wide and 10 feet high. Since me, Pete, and DJ were the only ones home (which was nothing new when real work needed to be done). Frank walked us out to the pile, about a 100 yards away. He backed up the truck and told us to load it up so he could take it to the dump. I really thought he was kidding but that son of a bitch was serious. There must have been 5 years worth of trash in there, including the rats and the dead pit bull. We started loading and after some 20 minutes, Pete threw down his shovel and started walking towards the house. I said, "Pete, where you going?" He shot back, "Fuck this shit, I'm going to call my Mom and tell her to come get me, this is bullshit." I said, "Ask her if I can stay with you guys until I get on my feet." So he went straight to the house. He returned 15 minutes later and said, "She said alright Coach, let's go get packed." Now I knew he was bullshitting like spoiled kids do, but I didn't care. I wasn't going to get bit by one of those cat-sized rats so we went and started packing. Once we were packed, we went out to the trash pile and said goodbye to DJ, then waited at the gate. When Pete's Mom, Debbie, got there we ran to the car. When we got in the car Pete said, "Coach is gonna come over for a while." I knew for sure now that she hadn't agreed to let me stay with them. But this was my wave, the door that Jim spoke about, so I just looked back at the home and smiled.

We drove to Pete and Debbie's condo in El Centro. I took a shower then watched some T.V. After a couple of hours Pete wanted to go over to his Dad's house. Debbie drove us over there and we went in. This house was as small as a tool shed and smelled like one too. We sat down and I said to Pete, "Dude, your Mom never agreed to let me stay at her house, huh?" He said, "Don't worry about it Coach, she'll let you stay. It's not like she's gonna let you sleep on the street." I said, "OK, because I'm not going back to that home, New Creations, or any other fuckin work farm. Because that's all they are. I won't let them bastards break my spirit, that's how I got here in the first place." Pete said, "Let me call her right now." He went into the bedroom, it was about four feet away from me but there was a bed there, and he called Debbie. I could tell it wasn't going good as I ear hustled the conversation. Pete got off the phone and said, "Bad news Coach, my Mom's being a bitch and she's coming back over here to pick you up. She says she'll take you anywhere you want to go." So I just sat there trying to think of some place that I could stay. Of course, I drew a complete blank. When Debbie arrived she asked me, "Coach, where can I take you? I said, "Debbie, I don't know. I've pretty much racked my brain and I've come up with nothing." She said, "Listen, I'll put you up in a motel for 3 days, but that's all I can do." I thanked her and grabbed my bag. I was literally living day to day. But I also felt the Lord was by my side and He would provide a way for me to survive. We got to the motel and I checked in. I hugged Debbie again and thanked her once again. She pulled out $30.00 and gave it to me. I said, "You don't have to do that." She replied, " Well, you have to eat." I humbly accepted it and turned and walked away. They left and I climbed the stairs to my room. I walked in and sat on the bed. That old familiar conversation began playing in my head. What are you going to do? You have 3 days and then what? This is bad, it's really bad. This isn't going to turn out well. I hit my knees before it could go any further and I prayed, "Lord, your son is in trouble, big trouble. I know you didn't want me to stay in that pig pen home and I know you have a plan for me. Please show me what I should be doing now. Guide my way and give me the courage to do exactly what you want me to do. Please take away this awful anxiety and fear. You tell us not to fear in your word, but I would be lying if I said I wasn't scared. I place my life in your hands and ask only for your direction. In Jesus Holy name, Amen." I spent the next 3 days doing nothing but fasting, praying, and calling my Dad. I left numerous messages for my Dad, but he wouldn't pick up the phone. I guess the caller I.D on my Dad's phone gave the number of the motel and on the third day, my last day, my brother called. I told him the position I was in and he agreed to call Dad and try to persuade him to let me in. He called back about a half hour later and said Dad was not going to budge. I thanked him for trying and hung up. It was getting late so I made a few more calls to Dad, begging and pleading for him to help me, on his answering machine. No luck. I got down on my knees and prayed again. When I finished I sat on the edge of my bed and meditated. I heard a voice say, "Go home." I looked around and no one was there. It was kind of scary but it was also good advice. I called Debbie and asked if she or Pete could give me a ride to San Diego. She said she would make some calls and get back to me. Well, that was a start. I then called my probation officer, Liz, and told her I was out of the home and that I wanted to go to San Diego. She said it was fine and to just call her when I had an address where I would be staying. I agreed to do that and I thanked her. An hour later, Debbie called and said she found a ride for me. It was Pete's ex-girlfriend who had remained close with his family. I packed up one final time and fell asleep. The girl, Monica, showed up at 10:00 am the next morning. We drove onto the 8 freeway west and I looked back and thought, "The hell with you Imperial Valley. If I never see you again it'll be too soon." I looked up at the mountains and I smiled. I was going home.

I had no clue what I was going to do if my Dad told me to hit the bricks. I was out of options, so I just placed the results in God's hands and prayed for Him to soften Dad's heart. But, if you want to get to the castle, you have to swim the mote. And I was swimming the mote. After a 2 hour drive we reached my Dad's house. It was good to see something familiar. I thanked Monica, grabbed my bag, and walked up to the porch. My Dad's car was there but he wasn't home. I was hoping he wasn't home and not just refusing to answer the door. I just sat down in a patio chair and prayed that the Lord would soften Dad's heart. I looked over at a grapefruit tree and saw the little birdhouse that Robert had made for Dad. It had a big B painted on it for Bobby. I began to cry as I thought about days of old. But I was home , and that made me smile.

I sat in the chair for an hour or so, then I heard a car drive up and I heard Dad's voice. He was saying bye to his friend Bobby, they had went to lunch. I was scared of being rejected, but I had nowhere else to go. Dad turned the corner and saw me sitting on the porch and walked up and hugged me. I could see in his eyes that he was crushed to see his son in the type of condition that I was in. Heck, from the last time he'd seen me I was now 50 lbs lighter, had a jacked up haircut, was wearing grubby clothes that didn't fit, I was unshaven because I didn't have any razors, my complexion was kind of ruddy, and I limped because of my bad knee. We cried for what seemed forever. We went in the house and sat down. I explained the entire story to Dad and he cried again. But after that, Dad shot into action. He took me to get a haircut and to Goodwill to buy me some clothes. He brought me home to take a shower. I scrubbed hard trying to get the Christian homes off of me. I was so glad to be home. From that day on, Dad would go out of his way to help me put my life back together. I spent most of my days sleeping and watching Christian programs like Joel Osteen and Joseph Prince. I was so programmed to not think for myself, and not go outside without permission, that I was kind of afraid to go outside. Going for a walk was a real struggle because I had this nagging feeling that I needed to get home. It was really frustrating. I made lists of things I needed to do but they would get all jumbled up in my head. I started making phone calls to get my food stamp and Medi-Cal cards transferred to San Diego county. It took over 6 weeks, and I had to jump through a lot of hoops, but I finally got my cards. I made an appointment with a doctor in Vista, Ca. for my knee. When I saw him, he ordered an MRI. After the MRI was completed, it was discovered that I had a torn ACL in my left knee. It didn't surprise me, because I knew for a fact, that a sprain would have healed in a year and a half. My next appointment was with a Psychologist to address my depression. I had been on anti-depression medication for over 20 years before I was arrested. In both of the Christian homes they believed you could pray away those types of disorders. I got back on the medications and began studying my Bible all the time. But after a month I realized that nothing had really changed except my appearance. And that really bothered me because Dad was really going out of his way to make me comfortable and trying to get me to open up. I just couldn't. I felt so hopeless and guilty, because I was being such a burden to my Dad, who was 79 years old. Plus my brother and my youngest sister were talking to Dad and telling him to kick me out. They don't think I know that shit. Well I do assholes! The walls in Dad's home are thin enough to where I could hear every word that was said. My family has always been dysfunctional but those motherfuckers are heartless. All of that just led to more anxiety and depression. My Dad told me that he was going to my sister's house for a couple of days to watch my nephews, while they went on vacation. I felt I couldn't take any more, so I began formulating a plan. When my Dad left to my sister's house it was time to put my plan into action. I went to my room and got the comforter off my bed and laid it down on the kitchen floor. Dad had left me money so I started to jump over the fence to go to the store. Just then I saw him pulling back into the gated community where we lived. I jumped down from the fence and sprinted towards the house. As I shut the door, he pulled into the driveway. I snatched up the comforter and put it back on my bed. Dad had forgotten his sun glasses, so he picked them up and left again. My heart was beating like crazy. I went back in the room and got the comforter and placed it back on the kitchen floor. I waited a few minutes to make sure Dad was really gone. I went back outside and headed to the store. At the store I bought a six-pack of beer and some pork rinds. When I returned home I sat on the couch and drank the beer and ate the pork rinds. When I finished, I knew it was time. The only thought I had was that I couldn't screw this up and look like an idiot again. This had to work. I picked up the bottle of

Ativan and went in the kitchen. I turned on the gas stove and sat down on the comforter. I had a glass of water sitting beside me. I took the top off the bottle of Ativan and poured them all in my hand. I picked up the glass of water and swallowed the handful of Ativan, washing them down with the water. There was no going back now! I laid down on the comforter and waited for this nightmare, I call my life, to drain from my body. Slowly I drifted off to who knows where, but I wasn't feeling any pain anymore. As I laid there comatose, Jesus appeared to me in the most beautiful purple robe that I've ever seen. For some reason I knew not to speak. I couldn't have spoke if I wanted to. I was in shock as my jaw dropped. He said, "Do my words mean nothing to you? I love you more than you can imagine and I promised to never leave you, is that not enough? My son, I know you are in pain and you are afraid of what will come in the future. Do not fear, the life that you seek is not far away. Put no faith in what others say, for they are not followers of my Father. Pick up your mat and continue the work that I've placed in front of you. You have great rewards ahead of you. Walk in hope with love in your heart, and that love will be returned to you in much greater measure." I awoke in a foggy haze. I stood up and stumbled around the house. It took me a while, but I realized that the gas was still on. I went in the kitchen and turned it off. I opened all the doors to let the house air out. I turned on the T.V. and looked at the guide. The time was 3:05 pm. I thought, wow, I slept for 24 hours because I took the Ativan at 3:00 pm on Friday. Then I noticed on the screen that it wasn't Saturday, it was Sunday! I was out for 48 straight hours. Then I panicked because Dad said he would be home around 5:00 pm on Sunday. I went in the kitchen and picked up the comforter and staggered to my room, bumping into walls. I made my bed and laid down. I remembered what Jesus spoke to me and it calmed my heart. That would be the last time I ever tried to take my life or do anything stupid like that. All fear and doubt left me for good. I wasn't going to let the evil one ever invade my mind, my heart, or my soul. I was anointed by the most high God and no matter what is going on in my life, whether it be people, places, things, or the evil one that roams like a lion seeking to kill, steal, and destroy... I was going to let the Lord fight my battles and just serve Him from now on. If people didn't understand my calling, well that was their problem. I was tired of letting my negative mind pull down my entire body, into that pit of despair. When my Dad returned home I told him what I had done and he looked at me with such disappointment. But I reassured him that I would never try a stupid stunt like that ever again. He seemed to believe me. When I prayed that night, I said, "Father, I am a very flawed man and I think I know what Paul experienced on his way to Damascus. Thank you for stilling my heart and showing me that the light at the end of the tunnel is not an oncoming train, but the path that you have for me. Guide me towards the light, and I promise I will follow it without ceasing all the days of my life. I am through dancing around you and giving you only a portion of me. You created me and I know you value me. I will never take for granted your grace and mercy. Please forgive me for stumbling once again. In Jesus precious name, Amen." Then I crawled into bed, and thought about that beautiful purple robe, and I smiled.

Things were starting to change for the better, but they were changing very slowly. I had been with my Dad for 3 months and the only things that I had accomplished was I got a California Identification card, had my Medi-Cal and food stamp cards transferred to San Diego, and I filed for divorce from Mitz. Once again, as I reviewed my life, I was at rock bottom. It was just a fact. I prayed all the time and I knew God had a plan for me. I just couldn't shake the awful depression and anxiety. I could tell that my Dad was worried that I was going to remain in that zombie like state. It became so overwhelming one day, that I looked at my Dad and said, "Dad, I need to go to the hospital. I'm a nervous wreck and I need help. My faith is strong but I need help with this paralyzing anxiety." My Dad said, "Sure, let's go." We drove to Tri-City Medical Center in Oceanside. I went into the Emergency room and checked in. When I saw the doctor, I told him what I had been through and I couldn't stop shaking. I was basically scared of everything. He diagnosed me as having PTSD (Post Traumatic Stress Disorder) and they immediately sent me to the Behavioral Health unit. I checked into the Psych Ward then hugged my Dad goodbye. I promised him that I would be open to anything they suggested to make me well. The hospital was nice and comfortable. I met with a doctor and he prescribed some medications. I immediately began the medications and I started to relax. The meals were good and the staff was very friendly. I mostly just slept for the first day. The next day my Dad brought me some clothes, razors, toothpaste, toothbrush, deodorant, soap, shampoo, and a hairbrush. That was a big deal for me because in my year and 3 months at the two Christian homes, I never had anyone to provide me with simple necessities. I was so thankful that I had my Dad on my side to help me out. I didn't feel like a loser anymore. Someone cared for me and had faith in me. I hadn't felt that for a long time. On the second day I was there, I had a counseling appointment. The counselor, Margie, was very kind and listened real intently as I shared my recent experiences. At the end of our session Margie said, "Eddie, you could do my job better than me. I'm not ashamed to admit that. You have a lot to offer society and the only thing it's going to take is time. Be patient with yourself, take your medications, and trust God to heal you completely. You've been through a lot, and it's going to take time for you to recover. Give yourself that time." I got up and hugged Margie. I told her, "I sincerely thank you Margie for your words of encouragement and your compassion. I didn't realize that I needed to hear those words. You've really helped me and I thank you." We hugged again and I went back to my room. As I sat on the bed, I felt this joy and peace that I had never felt before. When Margie said I could do her job better than she could, it really uplifted my spirit. Perhaps I could still be a counselor and help people recover from difficult times. From that day on, my confidence began to grow, and I was committed to recovering and growing as a person. Nothing was going to drag me down again, especially me. I was done projecting into the future, as well as dwelling in the past. Today was a new day, and I was going forward with my life. I participated in every meeting that the hospital conducted. I spoke openly and honestly every time I got the opportunity to share. I was leaving the past exactly where it belonged...in the past. My Dad came to see me every day and it was great. I told him what Margie said and he agreed with her. Before he left he said, "Eddie, you're too talented to get down on yourself." He began to cry but choked out, "I believe in you, you are going to make it. I don't know how long I can watch you beat yourself up. It just kills me. I'm sorry I let you hang down there in that hell hole, but I thought I was doing the right thing." I said, "It's OK Dad, I know you were just doing what you thought needed to be done. But know that I forgive you and love you." We both got up and walked to the door. We hugged and he left. He turned around and said, "Tell them to fix your ass soon, we got yard work to do." I just smiled.

On the third day, I got a call from a girl I went to high school with. We chatted for awhile but I didn't share much because I knew she didn't really give a damn about me, she was just sniffing around for something to gossip about. My only other call was from my best friend in the world, Robert Hock. He told me if I needed anything when I got out, just ask. I really felt good after that call. Someone besides my Dad really cared about me. I was sitting in the break room when a nurse came in and told me that the doctor wanted to see me. I walked to his office and said, "Hey doc, you wanted to see me?" He said, "Sit down Eddie. I have good news for you. We're releasing you tonight, so you might want to get your things packed. I've filled out all the paper work and the medications I want you to take. Please don't try to kill yourself with them, that would really piss me off." We both laughed and he continued, "I've written down where to pick up your meds and who I want you to follow-up with for counseling. Take care my friend, and the best of luck to you." I thanked him and went to my room to pack. When that was done, I went to the phone and called my Dad. I said, "Dad, I told them what you said about getting me fixed soon so I could help with the yard, and they told me to get the fuck out. So I need you to come pick me up." He said, "You told them that? I was just kidding." I said, " No not really. But they are releasing me tonight a 7:00 pm, can you pick me up? He said, "I'll be there." And we hung up. I just roamed around the hospital, talking to people, and reading. It was so cool to see people come into the hospital, crazy as a loon, and in a couple of days they would be completely normal. They do some amazing work at Tri-City. They actually are in the business of healing people that are suffering. I believe God makes places like that so that folks can get the help that they desperately need. Thank you Father for these places. It burns me up that places like New Creations and Heritage tout themselves as a place to find healing and restoration. When families send their loved ones there, they are under the impression that they will receive love, counseling, and support. Nothing could be further from the truth. They don't look at people as anything more than someone they can put to work and abuse. All in the name of God. It's absolutely sickening to me!

My Dad picked me up at 7:00 pm and we drove home. My Dad always drove me anywhere I wanted to go because I didn't have a driver's license, nor do I now. He would wait for me patiently, if I had a doctor's appointment, an appointment at Social Services, etc. I really appreciated that, and most of all, I knew I was loved. Two days later I took the bus to the library. I like the quiet serenity of the library. I went out to the bus stop to go home and sat down. As I waited for the bus, my Dad and his friend Bobby drove up. They stopped and I got in the car. Bobby said, "So Eddie, when are you going to get a job?" I said, "Well I need to get my knee fixed first." I'm pretty sure Dad didn't tell him about my hospital stay.

He said, "You better do something soon, because if anything happens to your Dad, I'll never forgive you." I said, "Whatever." Fuck him! Here I was, two days out of the Psych Ward, and he's grilling me like he was my Dad. Not to mention, he was clueless about the situation. My Dad just sat there and said nothing. He was placed in a real difficult spot, and I was sorry about that.

I needed to go back to El Centro one more time to pick up my belongings from Ralph at New Creations. I called my friend Lynward because I knew he had a truck. I asked him if he could take me down there and he said, "Sure." We decided to go on Saturday. Lynward arrived with his son Brandon and we took off to El Centro. On the way, I called Ralph and told him we were on our way. As we pulled into El Centro, I kind of got sick to my stomach. I hated that place with a passion. We stopped out in front of the New Creations home. I just stared at the home, remembering how abusive and oppressive it was. I went through the gate and knocked on the door. Ralph answered and took us into his tiny room where he had stored my stuff. We loaded up everything that I owned in the whole world. I thanked Ralph, and gave him a hug. I really appreciated that he had stored my stuff for over 9 months and not one item was missing. The boxes took up more than half of the space he had in that tiny room. I was humbled by his act of kindness. We got in the truck and headed back to San Diego. I was so grateful for Lynward's friendship. When we got back to my Dad's place, we unloaded the boxes and the trunks that held my baseball memorabilia. Since we hadn't ate yet, we went down to the store and bought a couple of pounds of cooked carne asada to make burritos. After we ate, it was time to go through the boxes. I was excited to see what the hell Mitz thought I deserved. A lot of things were missing like my shoes, my iPod, dress clothes, and my personal pictures. I didn't worry about that though, because at least I had some of my clothes back. Me, Lynward, and Brandon began opening up all of the boxes. I separated the clothes into one pile and my baseball memorabilia into another. I gave Brandon an autographed Reggie Jackson bat and a few other items. I gave Lynward a couple of jerseys to show my appreciation for taking time out of his weekend to help me. But that is how Lyn is, he is constantly helping others. I've said it before, I have the best friends and the best support network any man could ever have. I just had to swallow my pride and ask for help. Lynward and Brandon loaded their stuff up, and they left. I took a moment to pray, "Lord, thank you for providing me with such compassionate friends. Father bless Lyn and his family and let them receive the best that you have to offer. In Jesus Christ's precious name, Amen." A few moments later my Dad came out and looked around at all the stuff I brought home. He turned to me and said, "Ed, I can't believe Lynward drove all the way up here to Vista, from Chula Vista, then drove you all the way down to El Centro and back. I can honestly say that I've never had a friend like that. You are one lucky man, and that Lynward is one good dude." I said, "I know Dad, he's an incredible person, and the best friend anyone could possibly have. He's always been like that. And I truly appreciate him." We both shook our heads and smiled.

Lynward isn't the only friend that I've been blessed with. When it came time for me to go to court for my divorce, Robert paid for my attorney. I went into the divorce proceedings with such hope since I had an attorney, and Mitz didn't. Also, when I went to Family Court Services for my meeting with the mediator, I came away feeling confident that I would soon see my sons. The mediator seemed shocked at the things Mitz had done. Her history of mental illness was discussed, as well as her anger issues. The mediator met with Mitz and then with the boys. When I went to court the next time, the mediator's report to the court was complete. My attorney and I ripped it open and started reading it. Most of it was foreign to me, but I did see that they recommended both me and Mitz have a psychological evaluation and that Mitz was ordered to stop saying disparaging things about me to the kids. I learned that Mitz had told the boys that for the past year and a half I was in prison. She also told them to be on guard because I might come looking for them to harm them and her. Such bullshit! When we went into court, I sat with my attorney and Mitz sat at the other table to our left. Mitz had brought her fat ass boyfriend who looked like Shrek. He was one ugly motherfucker, but it was understandable because Mitz looked like a tore up crackhead. When court was in session, Shrek was sitting behind Mitz, coaching her every few minutes. Finally, the judge stopped and said, "Who are you sir?" Shrek said sheepishly, "I'm her boyfriend." The judge took off his glasses and said, "This is a courtroom, and I'm conducting this proceeding. If you say another word to Ms. Gonzalez, I'm going to have you thrown out of here. Do you understand?" Shrek melted in his seat. Basically, this is what was ordered by the court. I was required to begin reunification therapy before I could see the boys, I had to pay child support, and the restraining order was still in effect for Mitz, but was lifted on my sons. You would think that would be a good thing, but with the reunification therapy order, I wasn't allowed to see Mark or Robert. Nothing had changed. Without a job, how in the hell was I supposed to pay for the therapy? I raised them boys, and I know in my heart that if I had the opportunity to see them and explain the truth to them, we would be just fine. But like it or not, we were in the system now, and I had absolutely no rights to my own children. I walked out of that courtroom pissed. How could she continue to play this ignorant game? I'm a good father and everyone would agree to that. Yes, I had made mistakes, but should I have to serve a lifetime sentence? Man, there are child molesters out there that still get to see their kids after undergoing a few months of therapy. I couldn't understand why I needed therapy, hell I have a degree in Behavioral Science and Human Relations. It was all such utter bullshit. My friend forks out $3,000.00 for me to retain an attorney, and Mitz goes in with nothing but a bad haircut, and she gets everything. Do you think she has stopped speaking negative things about me to the kids? Hell no! But, at the end of the day, I was finally divorced from that hateful bitch. It was hard, but I smiled.

For the next couple of months, I saw three different orthopedic surgeons for my knee. They all agreed that I had a torn ACL, but weren't sure that I needed surgery. The bottom line was this: I had shit medical insurance through Medi-Cal and they didn't want to do the procedure. I was basically told to deal with it. Take Aleve every day, that was their advice. Hell, I wasn't looking forward to the 6 months recovery time, but I wanted it fixed. I had lived with it for almost 2 years now. I finally had a custom fitted brace that helps a little, but it's still painful.

I bought a bicycle at the Goodwill and started riding it everyday. It was great to get out and exercise, without my knee killing me. My legs were getting strong again and I started moving around a lot better.

I was learning the bus schedules, so my Dad didn't have to drive me everywhere. I decided that I needed to sell my baseball memorabilia. I needed to contribute more to our home. After placing a few calls around to different card shops, I found a guy in Mira Mesa that agreed to take a look at what I had. I got up the next morning and went through the trunks that held the memorabilia and sports cards. I got a medium sized box and placed some of the more valuable items in it. I borrowed money from my Dad and went to the bus stop. I rode the bus to Mira Mesa, which took about 3 hours. I found the guy's shop and went in. He was a real nice guy and he began going through the box. He was real interested, and he offered me $200.00 for the whole box. The items in the box were valued at $3,500.00, but I agreed to accept his offer, if he would also take a look at my entire collection. He agreed and wrote me a check. I told him I would return the next day with the rest of the stuff. We shook hands and I left. The next day, me and Dad loaded all of the remaining items into his car and went to the guy's shop. He looked over everything and offered me $450.00. Now, everything that I brought to him the last 2 days were valued at around $15,000, and he was offering me $650.00. I wasn't in any position to turn down cash, so I accepted his offer. I was happy because I gave Dad $250.00 and I had some cash for myself. I still had my food stamp card (called an EBT card) and I was able to contribute $200.00 per month towards our groceries. It felt good to contribute, even though it was just a drop in the bucket compared to what Dad spent on me.

Living with Dad gave us an opportunity to really get to know each other. We didn't have a bad relationship, we just didn't really know each other. Growing up, Dad worked every day and would come home dead tired. He would eat dinner, shower, and go to bed. So we really never spent much time together. Now, we were getting to know each other well. Dad would tell me stories about our family and it was so enlightening. I never realized how clueless I was about our family. We would get into some pretty heavy topics. Like his marriage to my Mom. My Mom was a lovely woman and I loved her so much. It was such a shock to all of us when she was diagnosed with cancer of the pancreas and lungs. It all happened so fast. Mom cooked Thanksgiving dinner in 2003, just like she always did. She was a fantastic cook. Anyway, she was her energetic and upbeat self on that Thanksgiving day. She was dead on December 13, 2003. How the hell does that happen? We all mourned the loss in absolute shock. I took it the best because I realized she was in a better place. I spoke at her memorial because no one else in the family could. It didn't really hit me until a couple of months later when I was driving to school and I realized that I would never see her again. I pulled the car over to the shoulder and basically just broke down. So when me and Dad would have our talks, I would ask him probing questions. He would answer them as honestly as he could. I told him that I remember him and Mom going into the bedroom and arguing. The thing was, Mom was usually the one screaming and yelling, and Dad would try to calm her down. I shared with him that it was like that with Mitz. She would be out of her mind, screaming, yelling, and threatening to take her life, that I never got to speak my position because I was constantly trying to calm her down so we wouldn't upset the kids. One thing I noticed was that she would always be able to control herself when we had her son Michael with us. She didn't want Michael telling his Dad that she was a downright nut. But if Michael was with his Dad, she would lose her fuckin mind, and she didn't care if it upset Mark and Robert. I will always resent that about her. It's the reason that I always pray that the Lord places a hedge of protection around the boys.

I really enjoyed my talks with my Dad and watching NASCAR together. I don't know how I got hooked on NASCAR, but I really enjoy it, especially with my Dad.

One afternoon I got the idea of getting back into coaching baseball. I went to Vista High School and met with the head coach. After a brief chat, he said he would like me to join his staff. I was overjoyed! All I needed to do was update my CPR/First Aid card and submit my fingerprints for a background check at the administration office. I was so happy that I rode my bike home at mach speed. I couldn't wait to tell my Dad. I ran in the house and told Dad, and he was real happy. I got on the phone and registered for the next CPR class available. Then I rode my bike up to the administration office, filled out the paper work, and submitted my fingerprints. I'm not stupid, so I was worried about the background check because I had been turned away before, and that was before I had a felony on my record. I just prayed about it and went to the CPR course a few days later. The following Monday, I turned in my certificate of completion from the course to the administration office. They said they would contact me as soon as the results came back from my background check. My Dad and I talked often about the possibility that I would be rejected because of my past. We both agreed that if it was meant to be, it would be, and if it wasn't, it wouldn't. Just stay in faith and place it in God's hands is what I told myself. One week went by, and I figured no news is good news. Two weeks, then three weeks past, and now I was worried. On the fourth week, they called from the Vista Unified School District and told me that I had failed the background investigation, and that they wouldn't be able to employ me. I kind of expected it, but I was still heartbroken. I was watching T.V. one day and I could tell my Dad wanted to talk. So I said, "What's up Dad?" He said, "You know, Thanksgiving is next week and I'm going to Tammy's (my younger sister) house and so is Charlie (my younger brother). You're not invited and I was just wondering if I could take you to one of your friend's house?" I said, "Don't worry about it Dad, I don't like any of those guys anyway. It would be uncomfortable." He was so relieved that I wasn't offended. See, I have two sisters and one brother. My older sister Pam and I get along great because we've been through some shit in life. My younger siblings are not my favorite people. They are arrogant and opinionated. Neither one of them has more than a high school education, and they suffer from personality disorders. But you can't tell them anything. In their minds, they are perfect, and that's just not true. Heck, I admit that I suffer from depression, but I do something about it. They believe, especially my brother, that it's everything and everyone around him that is causing him pain. It's self-imposed, period. So I didn't take offense, because no one can dispute that I have more friends than all of them combined. That's just a fact.

I was trolling around on Facebook one day, and I noticed a girl from high school named Tonya Rodriguez. She was two years behind, me but she always acted very mature. I was attracted to her, but I didn't think she would have anything to do with me because I had dated her friend. Not to mention, I had a girlfriend at the time. But I always thought she was so beautiful. That day on Facebook, I wrote her a message like, "Hey Tonya, still as beautiful as ever." She wrote me back and we just started talking. I gave her my phone number and told her to call anytime. She was so easy to talk to and her voice was so cute because she lived in Houma, Louisiana. She actually sounded like my Mom, with that southern accent. From that point on, we would chat about every other day. Whenever I would hang up with her, I would smile.

I began desperately looking for a job. I was willing to do anything. I started attending a church called Calvary Chapel in Vista. I went on Wednesday and Sunday religiously (no pun intended) and I really enjoyed it. It was great to attend church because I wanted to, and not because I had to, like in the homes. I would pray for God to give me a job, any job, that I could serve him. When it didn't happen, I figured maybe I was doing something wrong. Was it because I chewed tobacco, that I was offending God, and thus He was withholding my blessings? I struggled with that question, until it bothered me so much, that I made an appointment with Pastor Steve at Calvary. I sat down with Steve and explained my concern to him. He looked at me and said, "Eddie, so when I sit down at night and light up my cigar, I'm going to hell?" We both laughed and he said, "We all have are vices and society would have us believe that smoking or drinking prompts Jesus to run away from us. Nothing could be further from the truth. If God wanted you to quit chewing tobacco, He would put it on your heart so deeply, that you would have no choice but to quit. So if you haven't had that experience yet, just relax and serve Him to the best of your ability." I was so relieved when I left. Yes, I could serve God and still be a good Christian, all while chewing tobacco.

I picked up a little magazine on the way home from church, and noticed an add for people to gather signatures for various petitions. I called the number and spoke to a woman about the position. She told me to meet her at a bakery in Vista. My Dad drove me down there and I met with her. She gave a brief orientation and asked if I was interested. I said I was. I was to be paid $1.00 for every signature and I could work wherever and whenever I wanted to. She gave me a couple of petitions and sent me on my way. I stopped off at the local Rite-Aid and bought pens and poster paper. I went home and and made signs for my table that I was going to set up outside of the Albertson's grocery store across the street from my house. The next day, I set up my table, and began talking to people about the petitions. One was to have the three strikes law repealed in California, and I can't remember what the other one was for. I would spend 4 or 5 hours each day out there and I was doing pretty good. I would make about $60.00 for the four days I would work. It wasn't much, but it was a start. The important thing was that I was doing something. It felt good to have somewhere to go. But eventually, it sort of dried up because I would see the same people everyday and they had already signed. So I saw an ad for a telemarketer in Vista. I needed something close because I didn't have transportation. I applied with a company called NBR. They sold bumper stickers, key chains, pens, etc. by phone to retail stores nationwide. I was hired on the spot, and started the next day. I did really well the first week. I was the second highest producer in the office. I continued to excel and put up great numbers week after week. Around the fifth week my numbers weren't so good. I was really stressing because it was made clear that if you weren't producing, you would be let go. I got my sales up the sixth week, but the seventh week was brutal, and they let me go. I was disappointed, but not bitter, because they were honest with me from the start.

A news report came on T.V. one night, and they said police had found Junior Seau dead in his home from an apparent self-inflicted gun shot wound to his chest. I had become pretty good friends with Junior while I coached at Oceanside High. He would come around often and speak to the kids. He was a great guy with an upbeat spirit. The kind of person you want to be around. When he opened his restaurant , Seau's, in Mission Valley he invited me and my family down often and comped our meals. I was shocked to learn of his suicide, and couldn't fathom why someone with everything you could possibly want in life, would take their own life. It just didn't make sense. It was strange to think that when I worked at NBR, I was only about a mile and half from his house on the beach. I vowed that day that I was going to press on no matter what, until my blessing became a reality.

Since I had a little money, I would catch the Coaster in Oceanside, and spend the weekends at my friend Rick's house in Rancho San Diego. I would ride the Coaster down to Old Town and Rick would pick me up. We hadn't seen or spoken in many years, but when we got together it was just like old times. He was going through a divorce after 17 years of marriage. The fact that I had been through three divorces, allowed me to offer a little advice, and I reassured him that things would get easier and that his life certainly wasn't over. And he provided me with somewhere to go instead of sitting around at home. So it worked out for both of us. He had lost a lot of weight, so he would give me his clothes that didn't fit anymore. I was so grateful for that. Rick attended a church called Eastlake and they had very nice services. It was cool, because I could spend the weekends down there, and not miss church. On my way home from Rick's one day, I was sitting at a Trolley stop. A man that looked homeless rode up on his bike and asked me if I had a light. I told him no. He had a Mets t-shirt on and I told him, "That's a great shirt man. I've been looking for a Mets shirt like that. The only ones that I've seen are orange, but I want a blue one like that." He said, "I'll talk to you later, I need to find a light for this smoke." He rode off and I just sat there thinking how lucky I was to not be homeless. A few minutes later he returned with the Mets shirt in his hand, and he gave it to me. I couldn't believe it, he had went off and changed, and came back to give me the shirt. I was so humbled. I offered to give him a couple of dollars for it, but he refused. He said, "Wear it in good health my brother." And he rode off. What a kind man! It showed me that even when you don't think you have anything to give, you really can. I wear that shirt all the time, and I wouldn't trade it for the world. It means that much to me. I don't care that even after 15 washes, it still smells like Kool Filter Kings, I wear the damn thing.

I was missing my sons like crazy, so I looked around for a place I could get the reunification counseling. I found a place in Vista called The Art of Family. I made an appointment, and inquired about the cost. She said she normally charged $90.00 per hour, but after hearing my story she agreed to only charge me $75.00. Wow! I knew it wasn't going to cheap, but $75.00 was crazy. I went anyway, and for the three sessions that I attended, she never once mentioned my sons. I was paying for the sessions with the money I made working at NBR, and that money was running out. On the third visit, I told her, "Listen, the only reason I'm here is to get my sons back. I really don't want to discuss my ex-wife and her personality disorder. She means nothing to me, and she's not my problem anymore. I'm not here for marriage counseling. My only concern is my sons." She said, "We'll get to them soon, but I think we should explore your marriage and how your wife's disorder placed you basically in ruins." I said, "So how long until we address the reunification with my sons?" She said, "It will take as long as it takes." Our time was up, so I just shook her hand and left. My Dad thought it was a waste of money from the start, because I was only making minimum wage. I was starting to agree. He said, "I know it hurts son, but the right thing to do, is to wait until you are making decent money to pursue the reunification." I had to agree, but month after month, I knew Mitz was poisoning them further with her lies and bitterness. I just had to stay in faith and pray that the Lord would open a door for me and the kids to be together again. I just felt helpless. For God's sake, how long was this misery going to go on? I've paid my dues. My sons need me, and I need them. I just felt so weak and useless. Why the hell did I have to marry such an evil, bitter, and crazy bitch?!

I knew one thing, I wasn't going to give up living my life. Enough of the self-pity, depression, and gloom. I had to be at my best when I was finally back with Mark and Robert. It was time to start socializing with people instead of isolating because my life seemed worthless. I went out of my way to re-connect with friends and loved ones. A friend from high school and her husband offered to take me to a San Diego Padres game. Normally, I would have made up some excuse not to go, but I didn't. I went and had a great time. I don't think Lisa and Rick know how big of a deal that was for me. While at the game, I ran into two friends from college and they were so glad to see me, as I was to see them. Thank you C'Ann and Laura. I continued to grow as I attended Happy Hour mixers with friends from high school. I was becoming me again and it felt great. At the mixers, I had a chance to show people and tell people the truth about what I had been through. There were some rumors that were started by this big mouthed chick from high school named Tina. She was the one that called me when I was in the hospital. You really have to watch what you say to certain individuals. Especially when they claim to be your "good" friend, when in actuality, they are just people that went to the same school that you did. My friend Barb took me to her house for a fireworks display in Spring Valley. I had a great time, and it was so nice to see the old neighborhood. My Dad went with me to see an IVC basketball game against Mira Costa College, and it gave him the opportunity to meet my friends Coach Aye and Coach Robinson. I was having a blast being around old friends. I got in contact with a friend from high school named David and he had been through a similar experience with his ex-wife. I was sorry that David had to go through that, but it made me realize that I wasn't the only one in the world to marry a bitter, conniving bitch. These are just a few of the friends that helped me to get back on my feet. There are many more, but it would take another book to name them all. But you know who you are, and I thank and love you all. One of the most encouraging signs, that I was getting better, was that my sharp memory returned. There was a time there that I couldn't even remember my name.

I continued to go to church and pray for protection for my children, to find a job, to bring a woman in my life that I could share it with, and I even prayed for Mitz...That the Lord would soften her heart and that she would see what this was doing to our children. Most of all, I thanked God for giving me the best Dad a son could ever want. I know I've told you this already Dad, but I thank you and love you for putting me back together, after being broken in so many ways. I love you!

I didn't have a job, a girlfriend, my kids, any money, a driver's license, a car, and my knee still hurt like hell. But I didn't care, because I knew that I had a home, and Jesus was still on the throne. My friends were beside me and the Lord was guiding my every step. I continued to talk to Tonya just about every day. She is so intelligent, funny, and humble. Often times we would talk until 2:00 or 3:00 in the morning. It had been 5 months since we began talking, and I had told her everything about me, the good and the bad. And she still liked me. She accepted me, warts and all. One day I was riding my bike and I realized that I loved her. How could this be? We hadn't seen each other in over 30 years. As strange as it sounded, I knew for a fact that I loved her. That night, while we were talking, I told her I loved her. After a little pause she said, "I love you too, I've loved you since high school." What a relief! I knew I was taking a chance, but it worked. Now what were we going to do about it? I was in California and she was in Louisiana. We talked about me going to Louisiana or her coming to California. For me to go to Louisiana, it was going to take some time, because I needed to find a job so I could earn the airfare. She wasn't sure if she could get the time off work, so we were kind of stuck. We promised to pray about it and put it in the Lord's hands. After talking about it for a week or so, we decided that since I wasn't working, it would be best if I went to Louisiana. Finding a job in Louisiana couldn't be any more difficult than it was in San Diego, especially since I had no car. I said,

"So you're sure you want me to come?" She said, "Absolutely, the sooner the better." I said, "Alright, I'm going to ask my Dad for the money, then there won't be no going back." She said, "Get it done honey." I told her that I would call her back. I went into the living room and told Dad, "Dad, Tonya wants me to live with her in Louisiana." My Dad said, "When?" I said, "As soon as possible." He asked, "What do you need, money?" I said, "Yes, just the airfare." His eyes lit up and he said, "Go get my wallet off the dresser." I went and got his wallet, and he gave me his Visa card. From that moment on he was a man on a mission. It was night time, and he went out to the shed. I went and called Tonya, and told her it was a go. Dad came into the room with every suitcase he owned. I think he wanted to start packing my shit right then. I called the airlines and made my reservations. I would leave in two days. Dad didn't say it, but I know he was thinking, "Damn, you couldn't get anything sooner?" Before I went to bed that night, I hit my knees and prayed, "Father, you promised to pull me out of the pit and you did. Thank you. I'm sorry that I doubted you, but I promise to trust you always and forever. Please give me discernment in regards to this decision, and guide me to where I can be the most use to you. I praise you and I thank you. In Jesus Christ's holy name, Amen."

I spent the next two days saying bye to friends, and fending off their doubts. I was fully confident that the Lord had placed Tonya in my life, and I wasn't going to miss this blessing. The day before I was to leave, I packed up everything I could and placed the bags by the back door. I was ready to go. I didn't hardly sleep a wink, but when the alarm rang, I was up and ready to go. Dad gave me $200.00 and we were off to the airport. When we arrived, Dad pulled to the curb and we both got out. We unloaded my bags and just looked at each other. I said, "Dad, thank you for putting me back together. I couldn't have done it without you. I love you." He said, "We made it son. I love you too. Try not to fuck this one up." We hugged and I walked into the terminal. I boarded the plane and we took off for New Orleans. I remembered what me and Tonya agreed to on the phone. She said, "When we see each other, if I'm not what you want, just shake my hand. If I am, then kiss me like you mean it." I agreed. I was starting to get nervous as the plane landed. In no time we were at the gate. I grabbed my carry on bag and walked through the airport looking for my soul mate. I walked for a while, but I didn't see her. Finally I walked by a row of chairs, and there she was. I had walked by her, so I turned around and just looked at her for a minute. I walked in front of her and said, "Well hello." She stood up and I kissed her for what seemed like an hour. You know the kind of kiss that makes your back teeth float? It was like that. My lips were numb, but I smiled.

Today, Tonya and I live in Houma, Louisiana. I know without a doubt she is my soul mate and I'll spend the rest of my life with her. We are getting married on March 16, 2013 in San Diego on the beach. All of our friends have already agreed to come and it looks like it's going to be a great ceremony and a long overdue reunion for us all. I couldn't be happier! I got a job the first week I got there with the company that Tonya works for. I still have unpaid fines to the court, I still don't have a driver's license, and I still don't have a car. But we are happy together and we serve God together. That's what is important.

The only thing lacking in my life, is that I haven't seen or talked to my sons Mark and Robert for almost 3 years. I miss them so much. As I've mentioned before, I hope someone reads this book, and can offer help to gain my visitation rights with my sons. Maybe I wasn't the best husband, but I'm confident that I was always a good father. Nothing I've done has earned me a lifetime ban from my children. If you, or someone you know, can offer any assistance, please email me at eddierichey48@yahoo.com

For everyone else, if you are going through a tough time right now, please don't lose hope. There are brighter days in your future. Have the courage to seek help from those that love you. Even if like me, you feel that no one loves you, know that you are wrong. Just be honest with your friends about your predicament, and you'll be amazed how quickly they come to your aid.

And most of all, never doubt the power of our Lord Jesus Christ and His love for you. He never fails to provide exactly what you need each and every day. In my experience, the only people that don't believe in prayer, are those folks that have never tried it. So don't hesitate to send up those knee mails to the One True Living God. He will crown you with grace and mercy, every time.

God bless you and don't forget to smile!